Orchids for My Lady?
Roses for Your Dinner Table?
You Can Grow Your Own
In Your Own Home!

You can turn your indoor living space into a place alive with natural beauty when you make your garden grow with artificial lights. Whatever flower captures your fancy, whatever colors, shapes or textures you seek in your plants, Elvin McDonald tells you how to grow them, protect them from the various dangers of malnutrition, disease and insects that may threaten them, and display them in ways that will be a source of admiration from others and lasting enjoyment and pride for yourself.

ABOUT THE AUTHOR:

Elvin McDonald is senior editor and garden editor of HOUSE BEAUTIFUL. He is the author of several recent books: THE COMPLETE BOOK OF GARDENING UNDER LIGHTS; GARDEN IDEAS A TO Z; and with Lawrence V. Power, THE LOW UPKEEP BOOK OF LAWNS AND LANDSCAPE. He has written many articles, in addition to MINIATURE PLANTS FOR HOME AND GREENHOUSE, a book published in 1962. Currently, Mr. McDonald is directing the preparation of THE GOOD HOUSEKEEPING ILLUSTRATED ENCYCLOPEDIA OF GARDENING.

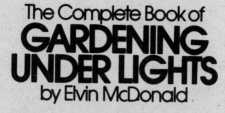

The Complete Book of
GARDENING UNDER LIGHTS
by Elvin McDonald

Drawings by Kathleen Bourke

The Popular Library Gardening Series
Elvin McDonald, General Editor

POPULAR LIBRARY ● NEW YORK

To my long-time friend and associate,

PEGGIE SCHULZ,

who introduced me to the wonders of

gardening under lights

CONTENTS

Acknowledgments

Many persons have helped me write this book. I think first of my mother, who allowed me to have a lighted garden in our home, and my dad, who assisted his twelve-year-old son in wiring and installing the unit. Over the years I have had the pleasure of visiting many under-light gardens, including those of Ernesta Ballard, Jean Boggs, the late Bernice Brilmayer, Elaine Cherry, Vera Dillard, Michael Kartuz, Ruth Katzenberger, Fay Scott Payne, Irwin Rosenblum, Peggie Schulz, Bruce A. Thompson, and Olga Rolf Tiemann.

A host of other friends have been helpful in the preparation of my manuscript, and in assembling the illustrations. Special thanks to Wallace W. Agey of Salt Lake City, who, upon receiving a questionnaire for *The Flowering Greenhouse Day by Day*, the book I wrote immediately prior to this one, wrote that he was not a greenhouse gardener, but a fluorescent-light gardener, and then proceeded to give me a full account; Pat Antonelli who provided me with an array of excellent photographs from which to choose; my associate Kathleen Bourke for her imaginative and helpful drawings; Robert Brilmayer, who assisted me in locating many of the illustrations made by his wife, Bernice, of lighted gardens she and I shared, admired, or designed together; Albert H. Buell, who called in a photographer to make photos especially for this book of his impressive greenhouse under-bench lighted gardens of African violets; Dr. Carl D. Clayberg, Associate Geneticist at the Connecticut

Agricultural Experiment Station, who provided information about his Connecticut Hybrid gloxineras; Mrs. Margaret Coon, former managing editor of the *American Rose Magazine,* who provided tear sheets of articles published about growing roses under lights; Howard Cross, Advertising Director of Lord and Burnham, who allowed me to adapt material that appeared originally in *Under Glass,* and who provided me with complete information about the Plantarium; Gordon W. Dillon, Editor and Executive Secretary of the American Orchid Society, who supplied me with a list of members who grow orchids under lights; Joan Faust, Garden Editor, who allowed me to use material I prepared originally for the New York *Times;* Charles W. Fischer, Jr., of Fischer Greenhouses, for photographs and helpful information; Lizeta Tenney Hamilton, Affiliated Chapters Chairman of the African Violet Society of America, Inc., who graciously provided me with outstanding photographs of her beautiful basement garden; Mrs. Armin C. Hofsommer, who first inspired me to try orchids under lights, and who, many years later, read and offered constructive criticism for the completion of my orchid chapter; Harold Johnson of Johnson Cactus Gardens, who provided suggestions about growing cacti and other succulents under lights; Mrs. Thomas B. McKneely for letting me study 35-mm. slides of her lighted plant cases for African violets; Larry B. Nicholson, Jr., who displayed great patience in achieving the illustration I envisioned of my FloraCart; Klaus Neubner of the George W. Park Seed Company, who keeps me posted on the latest developments in the field of phytoillumination research; N. Trumond Peterson, Garden Editor, who was kind enough to provide photographs of lighted begonia gardens; Dr. Sheldon C. Reed, hybridizer, who provided photographs of his basement garden; Star Roses for photos of miniature roses; Betty Stoehr, Associate Editor of *Gesneriad Saintpaulia News,* for information about her lighted gardens and a photo; Anne Tinari of Tinari Greenhouses,

ACKNOWLEDGMENTS

who wrote a detailed account of her experiences in growing African violets with artificial light; Mrs. Robert V. White for information about her under-light garden; Mr. Bruce D. Wiley, President of Tube Craft, Inc., who has corresponded with me over the years about the equipment and how-to of gardening under lights; and to Alma Wright, Editor of *Gesneriad Saintpaulia News*, who was immeasurably helpful in providing photos and in supplying the latest information about gesneriad culture under lights.

And again, as always, deepening love to my wife, Edith, and our children, Mark, Steven, and Jeannene, for the intangible ways they help me through the days and nights it takes to assemble a book.

ELVIN McDONALD

Kansas City, Missouri
1965

1

Light for Your Indoor Garden

As home gardeners, all of us are looking constantly for new plants, new methods, and new equipment that will help make the avocation more successful. The growing of plants by means of artificial light—a process called "phytoillumination"—is one of the most important horticultural achievements of this century. The concept has been with us for a long time—Liberty Hyde Bailey used arc lamps in 1893 to test the effects of ultraviolet rays on plants—yet, relatively speaking, this is a new method.

In the early 1950s the person who grew African violets under fluorescent lights was a pioneer. When Peggie Schulz and I founded the American Gloxinia Society and began to edit the *Gloxinian* in 1951, it was practically unheard of to grow gloxinias and other gesneriads by any other means than natural sunlight. By 1960 a phenomenon was apparent. Gardeners all over the world were growing all kinds of plants without so much as a single ray of sun beaming on them. In a decade phytoillumination had become a major way of gardening. Today we are only beginning to realize its vast potentials. New equipment and methods being tested now promise an even brighter future.

As I have assembled material for this book, three distinct groups of readers have come to mind. I have written first to the know-nothing gardeners. No offense is meant by this term. In this group I place some of my best personal friends. By the same token, I am a know-nothing electrician, yet I use and benefit immeasurably from electricity. The second group to which I have written are successful gardeners who will find phytoillumination a valuable aid in propagating seeds and plants and in growing flowers for the house around the year. My third group of readers are those persons who already garden indoors by means of artificial light. If you are in groups one or two, most of this book will apply directly to your pursuit of gardening without natural light. If you are in group three, it is my hope that in these chapters you will find new ideas, and inspiration for what must be a delightful hobby already.

Today, fluorescent lamps are the most popular source of artificial light for growing plants. The basic setup is a standard industrial, preheat fixture with two 48-inch, 40-watt tubes (one daylight and one natural white; or one daylight with one plant-growth lamp such as Gro-Lux) and reflector suspended about 18 inches above the surface of a bench or table on which potted plants are placed. When these lamps burn from fourteen to sixteen hours out of every twenty-four, most plants respond by growing compactly, luxuriantly, and by blooming well over a long season.

Controlled Light versus Sunlight

With phytoillumination plants are no longer dependent on the whimsy of the sun. In our area we often have several days of cloudy weather without so much as a hint of sunshine coming in the windows. Obviously, since plants are dependent on light for good growth, those growing in poorly lighted windows cannot attain the perfection that is possible in an artificially lighted garden.

Perhaps even more important is the fact that many dwellings simply have no well-lighted windows. Having lived my childhood days on a small ranch in western Oklahoma with hardly a tree in sight, all windows of the house glaringly bright nearly every day of the year, it came as a rude awakening when I moved to a city apartment in the East and found that the building next door cut off light from potentially sunny windows, and those that faced north were dismally dull. It was in such a situation that I first added a single 40-watt fluorescent tube over a windowsill and saw languishing houseplants turn into flower-show beauties.

With artificial light, then, it is possible to extend your indoor gardening area to any part of the house. A spare room. The basement. The attic. A heated garage. Part of a bookcase. Some writers have gone as far as to suggest using closet space. This sounds like a marvelous idea until you try to vacate a closet. But I believe that every person can find a place for an artificially lighted garden. In St. Louis I have seen an orchidarium in a renovated coalbin (see chapter 15); in the long, narrow basement of a Philadelphia townhouse I have seen a breathtaking display of gloxinias; and in the attic of a Levittown, New York, development house I have seen fluorescent lights used to illuminate 32 square feet of nearly ideal growing space for tropical plants and seed starting.

In 1950 when I first began to use fluorescents to supplement natural light under the benches of a small greenhouse, and over a plant table in a dark corner of my office, there was very little information published on the subject and even less equipment designed specifically for under-light gardening. Today manufacturers are producing an ever-increasing selection of lighted plant cases, carts, and stands —all to make indoor gardening an exciting and rewarding adventure. This book represents my experiences and pleasures with phytoillumination, as well as those of nearly countless friends and correspondents who garden better electrically.

2

Life-Giving and Sustaining Light

Plants cannot live without light. It influences rate of growth, formation of chlorophyll, leaf size, digestion, and other phenomena causing the plant to mature, flower, and produce seed. A working knowledge of how light affects plants will help you be more successful with phytoillumination.

Evergreen plants need light the year around. Most house plants, including African violets, philodendrons and coleus, belong in this category. Plants with thickened rootstalks, tubers, bulbs, corms, or rhizomes need light while in active growth. During the resting period they can be stored in a dark place where space is not at a premium.

Photosynthesis is derived from two Greek words meaning "light" and "putting together." Photosynthesis is the process through which the green leaves of plants, aided by light, manufacture sugars and starches from carbon dioxide and water. About 3 per cent of the total energy of sunshine reaching garden plants is used in photosynthesis. The remaining 97 per cent is reflected, passes through the leaf, or is absorbed as heat. Chlorophyll is the green coloring visible in leaves and present in all growing plants. Chlorophyll bodies, known technically as *chloroplasts*, contain the green pigment, the mechanism that is the center of photosynthesis.

The daily period of exposure to light affects the vegetative growth and flowering of many plants. This is known as *photoperiodism*, and was first designated as such in 1920 by

W. W. Garner and H. A. Allard, government scientists. While working with tobacco plants they found day length affected the flowering of the plants. Many scientists before them had experimented with gas arc lamps to determine the effects of added light on the growth and flowering of different kinds of greenhouse plants, but it remained for Garner and Allard to discover that plants can be divided into various groups, depending on reaction to day length.

Today, as a result of their discovery, we call plants that flower better when days are long *"long-day* plants." Tuberous-rooted begonias, calceolaria, and many garden annuals such as China aster are long-day plants.

Plants that flower when days are short are called *"short-day* plants." Chrysanthemums, kalanchoe, and poinsettias are popular members in this class.

A third group, called *indifferent*, are not affected by day length. African violets, tomatoes, and roses belong in this group.

Garner and Allard also discovered that day length affects height, bulk, length of internodes, runner production of strawberries, and the seed and bulb production of plants.

These were valuable findings. Knowing that long-day plants initiate flower buds by exposure to fourteen or more hours of light daily, growers can extend the day length with artificial light, thus bringing them into flower at any time of the year. Conversely, with short-day plants which initiate flower buds when days are short, that is ten to twelve hours, growers may force them into earlier bloom by shading with opaque black cloth. Artificial light used as a supplement to daylight will delay bud formation on short-day plants. However, a garden of short-day plants that receives no illumination except from fluorescent lights can be automatically lighted the proper number of hours daily for maximum bloom production.

Phytochrome is the name given to a newly discovered chemical pigment found in living plants. Light acting on this substance triggers growth changes through the life of the plant, from seed stage to maturity. Phytochrome is activated by red light, and tests have shown that a large percentage of plants mature more rapidly when exposed to long days of red light.

Kinds of Artificial Illumination

Several types of artificial light have been used to promote plant growth, but those most commonly employed are incandescent, fluorescent, mercury vapor, and neon. *Incandescent* light emanates from the well-known electric-light bulb. Its light comes from a tungsten filament heated by electricity.

Fluorescent light originates from tubular electric lamps, with an inner surface coating of phosphor or a phosphorescent material. Also inside the tube is a blend of argon and nitrogen gases and a minute quantity of mercury. When the gases and mercury are struck by electrons, the phosphor emits visible light.

Mercury-vapor lamps shed much more light than fluorescent or incandescent lamps. Similar to incandescent lamps in shape, they are impractical for home setups because they give off tremendous heat. The smallest size available is 400 watts, and its price is about $25.

In *neon* lamps the light is produced by an electrical discharge which takes place inside the lamp. These lamps are the familiar ones we see in advertising displays. The color of the light depends on the type of gas inside the lamp. Neon lamps are seldom used as plant lights except in limited scientific experiments.

Mercury-fluorescent lamps have glass bulbs similar to incandescent bulbs but the inside of the bulb is coated with fluorescent powder. Scientists and some professional growers use these to provide high light intensities and long-day conditions. For lighting small areas, 80- to 125-watt lamps are employed.

Get Acquainted with Angstroms and Millimicrons

Observe a rainbow and you will see a series of colors ranging from red to violet. This visible spectrum has wave lengths ranging from 3,800 to 7,000 angstroms. An angstrom is a term used to express the length of light waves. This minute unit of length is about one-two hundred and fifty millionths of an inch. Light energy ranges from 380 angstrom units for violet to 750 angstroms for red.

The average hobby grower need not concern himself with such figures, but with an increasingly large number of new agricultural lamps coming on the market, the terms angstrom and millimicron (a term used in measuring light waves) are frequently mentioned in describing the lamps.

Plant growth is dependent on wave lengths between 3,000 and 8,000, some of which are out of the range of the human eye. Where light is concerned, we humans think of it in terms of seeing. But plants use light in phototropism (turning growing points toward the sun) for elongation, flowering, and many other phenomena.

The visible part of the spectrum is only a small portion of the wave lengths emitted by electric lamps. At the short end of the spectrum are ultraviolet radiations, invisible to humans, but mighty useful in giving us a glowing tan. At the long end of the spectrum are the invisible infrared or heat rays.

With plants, the greatest photosynthetic activity occurs between 7,000 and 6,100 angstroms. The new agricultural fluorescents have been designed with particular attention to these wave lengths, their radiation ranging from 4,000 to 7,000 angstroms.

In the zone with radiation between 5,000 and 4,000 angstroms, the absorption of yellow pigments takes place. Important, too, is the second peak of chlorophyll absorption which takes place in this range. Yellow pigments are vitally important to plants for they trigger phototropism, the slow, steady, flowing motion of protoplasm, the living part of the cells, and the motion of chloroplasts. Warm white, white, natural, cool white, and daylight fluorescents emit radiant energy in the bands of 4,000 to 5,000 angstroms. Ultraviolet radiation with range of wave lengths from 4,000 angstroms is generally harmful to plants, but lamps of this type are useful for bactericidal purposes. Photosynthesis stops in both the ultraviolet and infrared zones.

Balanced Rays of Red and Blue

Many experiments have been conducted to determine the best type of artificial lighting for plant growth. All colors of lights have been used in an effort to simulate the spectrum. From thousands of tests, the finding of greatest importance to the gardener is that best growth and flowering is caused by red and blue lights.

Used alone, red light tends to make plants mature more rapidly. All red lights, or those exceptionally heavy in red, promote tall, spindly growth. Plants grown in incandescent light alone show these characteristics.

Plants grown under blue light tend to be short, with thickened stems and dark green leaves, but they exhibit few flowers.

To grow properly, plants need balanced rays of both blue and red. Fluorescents used alone are satisfactory for most of the plants you will want to cultivate in an underlight garden. Occasionally the addition of 10 per cent incandescent illumination is suggested, and these exceptions are noted throughout the book in discussions of specific plants.

3

Push-Button Solariums

It is possible to raise plants from seed to flower or fruit in areas where no sun or natural light reaches them. To make plants complete this cycle it is necessary to provide them artificial light with the proper balance of blue and red rays. Incandescents, abounding in red light, are not suitable for complete plant growth. These lamps have another drawback which is disturbing to home growers: They emit more heat than fluorescents. With incandescent sources the light drops off approximately as the square of the distance. If you move a plant *halfway* toward the lamp, you increase the light intensity *four* times.

The gardener who wants to improve the health of a few plants without going to the expense of installing fluorescents can use incandescents to supplement natural light. For example, English ivy, philodendron, or African violets on an end table will benefit from four to six hours of incandescent light supplied by a common table lamp with cylindrical shade. Incandescents alone are often used in the greenhouse as a light source for forcing bulbs, and for lengthening the day.

Incandescents manufactured especially for plant growth are available in sizes ranging from 60 to 500 watts. The reflector (R) and projector (PAR) lamps have reflectors built into the bulb. In our area it costs about one-third of a cent per hour to burn a 100-watt incandescent bulb. It has a work-life expectancy of 700 hours, but after 500 it darkens and emits less light.

Scientists have established that a mixture of fluorescent and incandescent light is beneficial to plant growth. This is accomplished by supplying a ratio of three fluorescent lamp watts to one of incandescent. One 25-watt bulb or three 10-watt incandescents will add about the right amount of this light to a pair of 40-watt fluorescents.

Some fluorescent setups come equipped with sockets for additional incandescent light. At least one firm sells an adjustable unit with sockets on either end and a pair of wires which can be bent so the unit is supported between a pair of fluorescents.

Fluorescents Promote Growth and Flowering

Although there are some sun-loving plants that grow best under a combination of fluorescents and incandescents, you will find it possible to grow most houseplants with fluorescent light alone.

White fluorescent lamps emit both red and blue light rays in varying amounts (see accompanying table). White fluorescent lamps are classified as warm white, de luxe cool white, soft white, natural, and daylight. The terms *warm* and *cool* refer to the amount of red coloring in these lamps rather than heat output.

APPROXIMATE RED AND BLUE LIGHT OUTPUT OF
FLUORESCENT LAMPS USED FOR PLANT GROWTH*

Type of Lamp	Red	Blue
Daylight	.5	3.2
Cool White	.8	2.5
Warm White	1.0	1.4
Natural	2.0	1.7
Gro-Lux, Plant-Gro	2.9	2.6

* From Shoplite Fluorescent Booklet H, Shoplite Company, 650 Franklin Avenue, Nutley, New Jersey.

Agricultural lamps such as Gro-Lux, Plant-Gro, and Plant-Lite utilize a blend of red and blue high-energy phosphors. In these lamps the green output has been reduced to increase the energy in the red and blue bands. They fit standard fluorescent fixtures. These lights emit a pinkish-lavender light, giving an entirely different appearance to pink and red foliage and flowers. Under these lights the most "washed-out" pink becomes vibrant, and the red colors fairly sizzle with color. So definite is the change in these colors that many aquarium societies have special show sections for fish and plants lighted by these special lamps.

No doubt these are but forerunners of many new kinds of lights which will be developed especially for plant growth. After most of the manuscript for this book had been completed, the Gro-Lux wide-spectrum lamps became available. Since I have not yet had an opportunity to test them, I quote from a Sylvania brochure: "Continuing research on radiant energy by Sylvania in this field has resulted in the development of a new phosphor blend which reaches farther into the far red area of the spectrum, producing extra values when applied to high energy crops requiring higher intensities.

"This is good news for, and represents an important contribution to growers of roses, carnations, gardenias, chrysanthemums, and all sun-loving annuals, as well as to such indoor grown vegetables as tomatoes and beans.

"Not only does this wide spectrum lamp energy source permit the commercial grower to produce more flowers in a shorter growing season, but also offers an extra degree of control in timing the fruition of plants to hit holiday markets at the peak."

If you have been growing plants under any setup involving white fluorescents and daylight tubes or other combinations which you have found satisfactory, your methods are not outdated. But if you would like, as it were, to see your garden through rose-colored glasses, or you feel your lighted gardens could benefit from a stronger concentration of blue and red rays, then by all means try some of these agricultural growth lamps.

A fluorescent lamp (other than the agricultural types) the same size as an incandescent lamp emits two and one half times as much light per watt. The heat output is the same but it is spread over such a large area of tube that it is much less noticeable. Thus, we say that fluorescent light is cool.

The region at either end of a fluorescent tube is called a *pole*. Light has a tendency to move in a curved line between these poles. The center 12 inches of tube are the peak of this curvature. This is the area which emits the strongest light. Here's the place to grow geraniums, cacti, and other succulents, gloxinias, and, indeed, any plants that prefer strong light. Use the end zones for lower-light plants or for propagating cuttings.

How to Measure Light

Before the advent of the special agricultural lamps we measured light for plants in foot-candles. Webster defines a foot-candle as, "A unit for measuring illumination: it is equal to the amount of direct light thrown by one international candle on a square foot of surface every part of which is one foot away." Light readings can be made with special meters, or, if you work with a photographic light meter, you can write to the manufacturer for a conversion table which will help you ascertain the amount of foot-candles your plants receive.

In my experience, it has not been necessary to bother with foot-candle readings. I can tell by the appearance of the plants if they are receiving the proper amount of light, and you can learn to judge this too. If plants need more foot-candles to grow to better proportions and to flower abundantly, these plants can be boosted closer to the lights or the lights can be burned longer each day.

Foot-candles are meaningless as a guide to the effectiveness of agricultural lamps. Light meters measure all light, and the agricultural lamps are lacking in green and yellow. The spectral energy distribution of these lamps is measured in laboratories with a spectro-radiometer. In our gardens we measure the spectral energy by the condition of our plants, moving them closer or farther from the lights as growth indicates.

Basic Fluorescent Setups

You need not be an electrician to install some basic and effective units. All you need do is purchase the unit complete with legs, reflector, and tubes, set it on a table, counter, or the floor, plug it into any household electrical outlet, turn on the switch, and you have light for a garden.

If you want a garden in the basement or any other household area you may want to investigate homemade setups which are easily installed. Before installing an extensive amount of light fixtures, check with the power company to see if your present electrical system can handle the extra load.

A pair of 40-watt fluorescents, 48 inches long, makes a splendid starter unit. These lamps are easily obtained for they are the same lights used to illuminate offices and homes. This unit will effectively light a garden area 2 × 4 feet. A pair of ordinary 40-watt fluorescents, with starters and a reflector, will cost about $20. You can switch lights on and off manually, but it is advisable to purchase a timer that will do the job automatically for you. Timers cost about $10 each, and it is not unusual to find as many as three at work in a basement-lighted garden of considerable size: one to handle the lights, one for the humidifier, and one for the circulating fan. Or, you can invest more money in a heavy-duty timer that is capable of handling a completely automatic setup.

If possible, purchase a 15-inch reflector with the tubes and starters. Smaller reflectors are not as effective in forcing the light down on the plants. If a reflector is not available, mount the lights on a section of plywood, which you should give two or three coats of flat-white, rubber-based paint for light diffusion.

Suspend the light fixture about 18 inches from the plant table or counter. Burn the lights twelve to eighteen hours daily, depending on the plants you grow. Flowering plants need more light than foliage types. Anchor stationary fixtures with chains; use pulleys for adjustable fixtures. The tubes can be a pair of the new agricultural lamps; one natural and one agricultural lamp; one daylight and one warm white; or other combinations of white fluorescents.

As your lighted garden expands you may want to add more lights. You can add single or "strip" tubes or pairs of tubes. Each 40-watt fluorescent placed close to the other tubes adds approximately 150 foot-candles.

If your growing area is large, consider the 74-watt, 96-inch slimline, single-pin type base tubes rather than 40-watt tubes placed end to end. The larger tubes shed an unbroken line of light while 40-watters placed end to end have a blank spot in the center growing area where the fixtures bump against one another.

Fluorescent tubes are available in 14-, 15-, 25-, and 30-watt sizes also, but most dealers do not stock them. If you can find the growing space, don't settle for anything less than a pair of 40-watters, for they are the most economical.

Both 20- and 40-watt fluorescents come in *preheat* or *rapid start*. The preheat are less expensive and they usually hold up better than rapid starters under humid growing conditions.

The Cost of Phytoillumination

The cost of operating artificial lighting varies in different sections of the country. It costs me about one-fourth cent per hour to operate two 40-watt fluorescent tubes. Life of a tube is about 12 months, but efficiency decreases as it ages. Replacement tubes for ordinary fluorescents cost about $1.35 each. The special agricultural lamps cost about a dollar more per tube. Use tubes with dimmed light for fostering a bench of foliage plants. Gardeners in warmer areas of the country often collect spent tubes and make greenhouses from them, and I know of several lath houses constructed from spent fluorescent tubes.

Ballasts sometimes burn out, and when this happens you will have a small repair bill. However, the expense in relation to the rewards of a fluorescent-lighted garden is practically nothing.

Portable Light Units

There are a number of portable units available for lighted gardens. Those suggested for table or perhaps floor display usually hold two 20-watt fluorescents. Some of them have adjustable frames and the reflector can be moved from 8 to 24 inches above the table surface. The bottom of these units is a rustproof plant tray.

The portable carts are real time savers. These have metal frames and two or three plant shelves. My three-tiered cart provides 24 square feet of nearly ideal growing space, as evidenced by color plate I.

Some hobbyists, particularly those who make some profit from their plants, have several of these carts in basement plant rooms (see color plate II). Other growers keep one cart to use as a propagating area, and another to use for displaying mature plants.

4

Decorative Lights and Planters

Growing is but half the fun of gardening; the other half lies in the showing. If you want to garden under lights you needn't settle for purely functional setups to illuminate your garden spot. Grow and show your flowers and foliage under decorative lamps or in well-designed planters, which you can buy or build.

Lamps for Added or Complete Light

When plants growing in natural light have weak stems, pale leaves, and few or no flowers, they probably need more light. Supplement natural light with daily doses of 4 to 6 hours of additional light from planter lamps or from other lamps you may be using in your home. Incandescent household sockets will accommodate a wide range of bulbs, from a 7½-watt, walnut-size globe to a large 200-watter.

Entryways, corridors, gloomy corners, stair wells, or recessed walls can become glowing garden areas when spotlighted by portable or stationary lamps. Add flair to a foyer by highlighting plants under an adjustable pulley lamp. Brighten a buffet, counter, or desk with plantings growing under lamps with cylindrical shades. Use surface-mounted 75-watt R-30's or 150-watt R-40's to shed light on potted plants or planters. Add clamp-on lamps to screens or room dividers, focus the lights on growing greenery, and the area will assume new importance. Change an ugly corner into a conversation piece with big, bold green plants illuminated by flexible wall lamps. Install fluorescent strip lights under valances to shed extra light on window-grown plants.

Versatile pole lamps with spaced lights and reflectors can double as daylight extenders for unusual ceiling-to-floor gardens. Train the lights on split-level room-divider gardens; focus them on a collection of gem-toned, colored glass, silvery pewter, or gleaming copper, and flowering plants or richly hued foliage; level them on small, plant-filled baskets suspended from a budget-wise bamboo partition; or train them on a potted manzanita branch bedecked with baskets of small begonias or African violets.

A slender 20- or 40-watt incandescent showcase light provides ample rays for a small shadow box bedecked with emerald-green foliage plants. Friends have handcrafted a pine planter that doubles as a sorter for family mail and a repository for a cream and green pothos. A 40-watt day-extender light keeps the vine in fine fettle, even though it receives dim daylight.

In a kitchen area receiving some natural east light, I saw a set of maple shelves covered with small pots of scented geraniums—nutmeg, peppermint, apple, and lemon. Bracket lamps with glass chimneys, used as four-hour day extenders, gave this lighted garden an early American touch.

A single potted plant growing under a desk lamp makes a pretty room accessory. Atop our piano in a dark corner I once grew a specimen plant of 'Merion Beauty' English ivy in a brass planter set directly beneath a small lamp with a 100-watt incandescent bulb that was burned from seven to twelve hours daily. When you have a heavily flowering plant deserving a place in the limelight, ensure continued bloom by giving it evening hours of light from any cylindrical-shaped table or desk lamp.

Desk lamps with single or double 15-watt fluorescents can

be used to light gardens of miniature plants, cacti, and other succulents, or to light one or two 4-inch pots of African violets. If they provide all the light these plants receive, burn them sixteen hours daily.

Circular fluorescents, available in 22- to 40-watt sizes are sometimes available with attached planters. These highly decorative units burned ten to sixteen hours daily foster the growth of numerous flowering or foliage plants. Try suspending one over a stainless-steel or brass Lazy Susan serving tray filled with small water-polished stones to hold moisture. Add small pots of miniature roses, wax begonias, dwarf geraniums, or African violets. Construct a suitable reflector to hide the fluorescent lamp and to direct rays on the plants. Hang from the ceiling with ornamental chain. Presto! You will have created a dramatic garden in the round.

Lighted Plant Cabinets

You can buy ready-made planter cabinets, have one custom made, build one yourself, or make a remodeled one from an old radio or record player cabinet, a bookcase, or a buffet.

We have owned lighted plant cabinets which fitted into a cramped New York apartment; a more spacious one for a house in the suburbs; a combination planter and bookcase that once doubled as part of my study; and a really magnificent glassed-in cabinet suitable for growing an infinite variety of eye-appealing gardens.

The lighted cabinets on the market are rustproof metal with a growth chamber measuring 24 inches wide, 26 inches high, and 19 inches deep. Four fluorescent tubes provide approximately 800 foot-candles light intensity at tray level. If the plants you grow require less light, you can remove one or more of the tubes.

My combination book- and plant-case is 51 inches long, 32 inches high, and 18 inches wide. Sliding glass doors help maintain humidity at a high level. This accommodates a pair of 40-watt fluorescents. A shelf with adjustable shelf standards is about 12 inches from the light tubes. Although I had the tinner make a galvanized-steel tray to fit this shelf, I often remove it and grow geraniums, for instance, with only pot saucers to protect the wood from water rings. I have found that geraniums are subject to a troublesome virus disease when the pot bases rest on a tray of moist peat moss or similar humidity-producing material.

A similar though smaller cabinet used in a friend's home doubles as an occasional table and a lighted plant cabinet. This unit is 28 inches long, 22 inches deep, 30 inches high, and also holds a pair of tubes, these being 20-watters. Glass doors keep humidity high, and a small rubber-bladed fan used at intervals during the summer keeps the air in satisfactory condition for the plants.

Making these cabinets is a good project for the hobbyist with power tools. Or you can have a cabinetmaker construct one to fit your space.

Attractive plant cabinets can be made from castoff console radios, televisions, music cabinets, or buffets. Remove the mechanical parts, paint the interior flat white for better light diffusion, install fluorescent lights, and you have the makings of an effective under-light garden.

A friend who ran out of propagation space made such a cabinet out of a discarded music cabinet. He removed the back of the cabinet for air circulation, but left the doors on the front so that, when it faced the room, no one was aware of the dozens of plants being rooted inside.

One popular place for either open or glassed-in fluorescent-lighted cases is the counter-top area under kitchen cabinets. Usually one 20-, 40-, or 74-watt fluorescent tube is ample lighting, depending on the length of counter-top area available or desired for gardening. If there is room, the installation of two tubes, running parallel, should result in high light intensity and the successful culture of flowering plants such as African violets, gloxinias, and begonias. Several illustrations in this book show kitchen-cabinet counter-top planters.

One greenhouse firm manufactures an attractive glass case, complete with fluorescent lights, and called a Plantarium. So handsome is this case that friends use one in a foyer to show off a collection of rex begonias growing under agricultural lamps. It would also be ideal for growing other begonias, African violets, gloxinias, miniature orchids, or just about any other plants you like. Venturing beyond the realm of these more or less common plants, I would suggest for the Plantarium any of these: bertolonia, calathea, chamaeranthemum, fittonia, maranta, stenandrium, *Cissus striata*, *Ficus repens*, and *F. radicans variegata*, *Pteris ensiformis victoriae* (silver and green fern), episcia, hypoestes, impatiens, pellionia, plectranthus, *Scilla violacea*, and *Siderasis fuscata*.

Lighted Miniature Greenhouses

Many firms manufacture miniature greenhouses in sizes ranging from 12 to 20 inches in length. All have waterproof planting areas, and clear plastic domes. Some have heating cables to speed propagation. At least one firm gives purchasers an option on having the greenhouse equipped with fluorescent lights.

If you use incandescent or fluorescent lighting to give plants extra illumination, keep the lights close to the dome, but do not let them touch the plastic. Incandescents, with their higher heat level, may prove too hot for small seedlings when used inside a closed unit.

Armed forces careermen and their families, ever on the move, learn to live in a wide variety of quarters. But no matter how small the house or mobile home, you cannot keep a good gardener from finding space for plants. One service family of our acquaintance designed a miniature greenhouse which goes with them on all their travels. You can easily construct a similar unit. Purchase sheets of clear plexiglass from a plastics dealer. Saw them to size for four sides, a bottom, and a top. Glue together with any waterproof plastic adhesive. In a house with little natural light, this miniature garden may be illuminated by aiming a fluorescent-tubed desk lamp over the roof. Inside you can grow miniature gloxinias, jewel-toned rex begonias, or unusual tropical foliage plants such as bertolonia.

Electrically Lighted Office Gardens

Strategically placed plants in offices and other public buildings create a sense of motion, a feeling of closeness to nature, and a delightful atmosphere. Lighted greenery will add liveliness to otherwise dark corners, and planter boxes anywhere may be highlighted by indirect lighting or spotlighted in the glow of recessed ceiling lamps.

If office plants receive strong rays of natural light, then whatever supplementary artificial illumination they receive will be beneficial. However, if plants receive no natural light, then all flowering kinds, and most foliage types, in order to thrive, need the usual number of foot-candles of artificial light, just as if they were being cultivated by phytoillumination in a home setting. In many situations it is possible to design fluorescent-lighted office gardens with the fixtures recessed out of sight above, and a tray recessed into a planter box, wall, or the floor below. If the pots are inserted in moist peat moss, contained by the tray, and the lights turned on and off automatically by a timer, this kind of garden will require very little maintenance. All will agree

Figure 1. Artificially lighted wall garden makes handsome room-divider. Two 20-watt, 24-inch fluorescents are recessed into wall above each of these 20-inch planter niches. Roots of plants are in small pots buried to the rim in moist peat moss contained by plastic window boxes set into wall.

that a garden of real plants is far more appealing than a collection of unchanging artificial foliage and flowers.

An artificially lighted wall garden could be an exciting addition to an office or home. Step one is to construct a false wall of plasterboard, pegboard, or plywood, and cut alternate square niches into it to accommodate pairs of 20-watt fluorescents, or rectangles for 40-watt tubes. Add metal or plastic planter bins and place plants so the pot rim is just below the bottom of the niche frame. Plant these "shadow-box" pictures with a variety of flowering and foliage plants—African violets, begonias, peperomias, fittonias, and episcias make a good showing. Add trailers such as variegated English ivy, philodendron, and cissus. Train some of the vines up, let others trail in a design fixed by training the stems with tape or pins.

Complete plans for three different indoor planters that make use of fluorescent light have recently been published by the United States Department of Agriculture. One is principally a decorative accessory in a room, one is for displaying plants in hanging baskets, and the third can be used as a room divider or in a dimly lighted corridor. The units are designed for use with panel fluorescent lamps from General Electric and 110-watt VHO fluorescent lamps from Sylvania. Single copies of this publication, "Indoor Garden for Decorative Plants," may be obtained free on postcard request to the Office of Information, U. S. Department of Agriculture, Washington, D.C. 20250.

5

Phytoillumination Primer

When you garden under artificial light you are in complete control. You can give your plants a steady stream of life-giving rays even in the darkest, cloudiest winter months. But artificial light is not a panacea for all plant ailments. It is the one all-important factor around which you can build satisfactory conditions of temperature, humidity, and culture, including a suitable growing medium, proper watering and feeding.

In some instances intensity of light increases the number of flowers. Light can even change the color of flowers and leaves, adding brilliancy to flowers and deepening the color of leaves. Conversely, applied too liberally, light can also bleach flowers and leaves. Light can bring exquisite form to foliage and flowers or used unwisely it can cause abnormal growth such as bud and foliage malformation.

If you have successfully grown plants in window gardens, you can keep most of your growing methods and become an even more successful under-light gardener. If you are a novice, be grateful, for you can learn indoor gardening techniques the easy way. If you are among the multitude of gardeners striving to keep stringy plants alive and rejoicing when a stray bloom appears, you will be thrilled with this marvelous way to garden.

How Much Light?

Plants in outdoor gardens and greenhouses often receive illumination as high as 10,000 foot-candles at noon on a summer day, to a low of 900 foot-candles on a gloomy December day. In the average window garden with a southern exposure, foot-candles may peak at 8,000 in early summer, to less than 200 on a north windowsill in December. The light output at the center of a pair of 40-watt tubes, 5 inches below, is 500 foot-candles.

While scientific laboratories devote much time and space to studying the effects of artificial light on all manner of field crops and even weeds, very little scientific data is available on the growth and development of the hundreds of kinds of ornamentals we like to grow indoors. There is one exception: African violets grown under controlled light and other conditions have been studied at many universities. Scientists have found these plants need 300 to 600 foot-candles of light to complete their growth cycle. Their growth requirements change with age. Seedlings need a greater quantity of light than mature plants. Blue-flowered types need more light than white- and pink-flowered ones.

African violet light requirements can serve as a guide to growing many other favorite plants—gesneriads, besides the saintpaulia or African violet, including gloxinias, most begonias, ferns, azaleas, cyclamen; colored-leaved foliage plants such as coleus, many orchids, and dozens of other plants.

If you are planning a basement or closet garden, paint the walls and ceiling white for better light reflection. Use a flat-white, rubber-base paint. Mirrors in the background and at the ends of a growing section serve a double purpose; they reflect the light and also serve to make your garden look twice as large. Shiny aluminum tins used as pot saucers help deflect light onto lower leaves.

Have you ever noticed how dim your car's lights grow when the lenses are dirty? The same thing can happen when light tubes get dusty. Liquid used for cleaning windows does a fine job cleaning the lights. Remove them from the fixtures and clean all around.

Aging lamps emit less light. They first show signs of aging by growing darker at the end zones.

If you want to grow a collection of tall plants such as potted fruit, consider using the regulation horizontally suspended lights above them and vertical tubes at the ends of the lighted area.

Seedlings and young plants needing maximum light can be placed from 1 to 4 inches from a pair of 40-watt lights. Here they receive approximately 600 to 1,000 foot-candles of light.

Older plants can be spaced with a distance of approximately 11 inches between the tube and the rim of a 4-inch pot.

Light intensities will vary greatly with the wattage and number of tubes you are using. To give you an idea of the number hours of light duration plants need daily, start with twelve to sixteen hours out of every twenty-four for African violets and similar tropicals. Some growers give geraniums and certain orchids as much as eighteen hours light per day.

Through observation, check the effect of light on your plants. If normally flat, compact-growing plants such as African violets and gloxinias start growing like a stalk of celery, with leaves pulling toward the light, or if stems weaken and let the plant trail over the edge of the pot, these plants are not receiving enough light. Boost them closer to the lights. An inverted pot makes a good booster. If this fails to help the growth, burn the lights longer each day or change from small 20- to 30-watt tubes to larger tubes.

Plants showing bunched leaves and hard centers may be receiving too much light, though this symptom may indicate an attack of cyclamen mites. Likewise, leaves showing loss of color and burned areas are also getting more light than they need. The answer to these problems is obvious; move the plants away from the lights or move them from the center of the lights to the end zones where light is less intense. Or burn the lights fewer hours daily.

What happens when you want to move a plant from an artificially lighted area to natural light? Nothing spectacular if the plant receives as much light from natural sources as it did from the electric lights and if the humidity in the new growing area is as high as in the plant room or case. Plants growing under artificial light are somewhat more tender than those growing at a sunny window, so condition the plants you move by starting them at a light north window or in another area where the lush leaves won't receive a barrage of burning rays. Within a few days they'll be able to make the transition to the sunshine without damage to leaves, providing, of course, that the plant is a type which grows well in full sun.

I like to bring the best of my flowering and foliage plants into the living room or dining room for temporary decoration. As flowers fade they are returned to lighted setups to be replaced with other plants which may be just entering a blooming cycle.

Vacation Care

If you have an outdoor garden, consider vacationing many of your houseplants in sheltered areas. African violets have such tender leaves and such an affinity for all kinds of mites that they are usually safest left in the house around the year.

Before setting *any* artificially light-grown plant in the

outdoor garden, condition it so that there is less shock from the drastic change in light, temperature, and, probably, humidity. Hardening off is the term most gardeners use for this practice. Move the plant to a naturally lighted area such as a porch having lower temperature than that in the artificially lighted growing area. Decrease the water supply somewhat to give the plant tissues a chance to harden. Place such plants in a sheltered garden area under a shrub or in a lath house for a while. Sun-loving plants such as geraniums soon become acclimated and can be placed in full sun. Most begonias, other than the obliging semperflorens, must have some shade during this vacation period.

Before returning plants to indoor growing areas, spray them with insecticide such as malathion or an aerosol of houseplant pesticide.

If you are vacationing and do not have a reliable person who volunteers to tend your plants in your absence, water them by setting pails of water above the plants and running heavy cords from the pail to the soil. If this isn't feasible, slip a plastic covering over the plants. This retards evaporation, and your plants may not need watering for a week to ten days.

Watering and Fertilizing

Learning to water plants correctly is something you really have to discover for yourself. How much water a plant needs and how often it needs watering depends on the type and size of plant, the kind of pot it is growing in, the soil, temperature, and humidity.

Gift plants such as calceolaria, hydrangea, and cyclamen need copious watering. Best way to do this is to give them a weekly soaking in a bucket of water, then daily watering. Cacti and other succulents need less water than thin-leaved plants. Flowering plants growing in potbound condition need watering more frequently than plants of the same size growing in larger pots. Plants growing in clay pots need watering more often than those in ceramic, plastic, or metal pots. Plants growing in hot, dry air need watering more often than those in cool, moist air. Sandy soil dries out faster than clay soil. Soil rich in humus, such as leaf mold or peat moss retains water well but it must never be allowed to become completely dry so that it shrinks from the pot sides. This is detrimental to the plant and the soil is difficult to re-wet.

You can buy a watering gauge which will help you judge a plant's moisture needs. Operate this by sticking the point in the soil and reading the top of the gauge. I much prefer the old reliable rule which says, "Touch the topsoil and if it feels dry, it's time to water." Follow this rule for a while, and before you know it you'll be able to judge moisture needs by the appearance of the growing medium at the surface. Until you become familiar with your plants' water requirements, test such plants as African violets, other gesneriads, and miniature roses, among others, by poking your finger about a half inch into the soil. If it feels dry at this level, you can be sure it's time to water.

Use room-temperature water and water thoroughly from the top or bottom. Or alternate, watering from the top one time, from the bottom the next. If you grow many plants you can save time by keeping them in a waterproof tray of metal or plastic. There are handy gadgets for watering plants growing on high shelves. I use the watering aid manufactured by Tubecraft of Cleveland. It consists basically of a slender plastic tube with cutoff for easy start and stop to control the flow of water from one pot to another. The base of this unit is inserted into a pail of water hung from a hook in the basement ceiling, thus completing the siphon setup.

Try not to spill water on the crowns of budded gloxinias,

African violets, calceolarias, or plants similar in habit, or rot may set in.

Clean furry leaves with a soft camel's-hair brush or take them to a sink and wash the leaves with tepid water. Of course this is a good treatment for all smooth-leaved plants. If you like highly polished leaves, keep them glossy with Schultz Plant Shine liquid or a similar product.

How and When to Fertilize Plants

Fertilizing plants is a near ritual with some growers. Others fertilize *all* plants at stated intervals without too much regard for the individual plant and its needs.

Generally, growing plants thrive on biweekly feedings of soluble fertilizer. Any of the well-known brands such as Hyponex, Plant Marvel, Blossom Booster, fish emulsion, Ra-Pid-Gro, or Ortho are good. Before fertilizing, check topsoil to see that it is moist. Fertilizer poured onto dry soil may burn the feeder roots and cause the leaves to droop over the edge of the pot. Withhold fertilizer from plants during any period of rest or dormancy.

Some growers like to alternate types of fertilizer, applying a chemical for one feeding, an organic type for the next. For example, you might alternate Ra-Pid-Gro and Atlas Fish Emulsion.

Many of my friends report great success using Blue Whale, a combination of shredded moss, seaweed, and ground whale parts. This is sprinkled on the topsoil, then watered in.

Ample Humidity Does Wonders

Flowering plants grow best when humidity is at 40 per cent, and preferably in a range of 50 to 60 per cent. You can measure humidity with a hygrometer obtainable from plant suppliers or hardware stores. This inexpensive instrument measures humidity (the moisture in the air) just as a thermometer measures and records the temperature. A hair hygrometer costs more but is much more accurate than one that depends on paper.

There are many ways to increase the humidity around your fluorescent-lighted garden. Grow plants atop a tray or saucer of moistened vermiculite, pebbles, or green sheet moss. The green moss is obtainable on order from florists and it gives plants a natural-looking foundation—like a carpet of green grass.

Set glasses of water among your plants or place potted plants on bricks sitting in water.

There are many kinds of fogging devices which growers use daily or several times a day to keep the air moist. Check your hygrometer in the morning. If relative humidity is less than 50 per cent, use warm water to mist the air surrounding your plants, and fog them until beads of moisture are visible on all foliage.

Electrically operated humidifiers are a real boon to indoor gardening success. Even a gallon-size one will raise the humidity in a small plant room. Select a cool-vapor type, and preferably one with a humidistat. Since our home has been centrally humidified, we can keep the humidity between 40 and 50 per cent and feel perfectly comfortable in the winter with temperatures at or slightly under 70 degrees.

If you want a fluorescent-lighted basement garden, and do not want to attempt humidifying the entire basement, you can quickly and inexpensively install walls of polyethylene plastic. Add a cool-vapor humidifier and humidistat, a small circulating fan to keep the air moving, and your basement greenhouse will be complete. If you burn several fluorescent units inside, they will produce enough warmth to put the average basement temperatures into an ideal range for most pot plants.

Temperature and Ventilation

Daytime temperatures which are comfortable for you are suitable for most houseplants, that is 68 to 80 degrees F., with a drop of 10 degrees at night. If the plants you want to grow require lower temperatures, you will have to find cooler growing areas such as a spare bedroom where the temperature can be lowered, a porch, or perhaps a basement area.

Good ventilation is essential to plant health. Plants growing in our living room, for instance, receive enough fresh air during the winter through the children's many comings and goings. Be sure, however, that cold, drafty air never blows directly on your plants. Some African violet enthusiasts recommend letting fresh winter air into other rooms in the house to let it warm, then opening the door to the plant room and admitting the warm, fresh air. Plants growing in poorly ventilated basements or attics may need the benefit of a fan or two to keep the air circulating. Some growers report success when they have installed an exhaust fan in a basement window, in addition to other fans that circulate the air.

A fluorescent-lighted garden enhances the many pleasures of being in this room of fine books and recordings. Two 40-watt lamps provide ample illumination for rhizomatous or star begonias and African violets in abundant flower around the year. The elegant table lamp provides supplementary incandescent light for African violet and begonia that receive some natural light. (ROCHE)

Basic setup for growing plants under fluorescent light: 48-inch reflector unit with two 40-watt tubes. Photographed by Sam Caldwell in the Nashville, Tennessee, home of Jean Boggs. Plants include episcias, *Begonia foliosa*, smithiantha, achimenes, begonias, sansevieria, and pothos. Miss Boggs' light-garden favorites include episcias 'Jean Bee,' 'Tri-Color,' and 'Moss Agate,' begonias *foliosa*, 'Verde Grande,' 'Maphil,' and 'Virbob,' and two achimenes, 'Cettoana' and 'Peach Blossom.'

Tabletop lighted garden from Crafthouse Manufacturing Company provides growing space for flowering African violets and miniature rose, with coleus and variegated English ivy for foliage accent.

Tropical beauty surrounds goldfish pool camouflaged by bricks in Bayside, Long Island, house. Featured plants include avocado tree at left, rex and semperflorens begonias, episcias, ferns, *Ceropegia woodi* (rosary vine), and dwarf palm. (BRILMAYER from *The Begonian*)

Betty and Charles Stoehr in Greenwood, Indiana, basement garden from which many sweepstakes-winning African violets have originated. Mrs. Stoehr's newest tables are 30 x 60 inches, mounted on rollers, with lights 15 inches from the tabletop. These are burned fourteen hours daily, lighted either with warm white or Gro-Lux fluorescent tubes; Mrs. Stoehr does not recommend daylight tubes for African violets.

Every day is a flower show in these fluorescent-lighted plant carts adjoining a dining area. Here the specialty is African violets grown to prize-winning perfection, but practically any of the hundreds of plants discussed in this book could be cultivated in units like these. (GOTTSCHO-SCHLEISNER, INC.)

6

Soil, Containers, and Potting

Plants confined in containers need soil or some other substance in which to anchor roots. Usually it is from this material that the plant will derive most of its food. Good garden loam consists roughly of about 35 per cent sand, 25 per cent clay, 10 per cent organic material, and the balance in moisture and air. Soil such as this with a mixture of both fine and large pores allows free drainage, yet has an ideal water-holding capacity.

Soil too heavy in clay will puddle and drain poorly; too sandy soil drains freely and dries out rapidly. Organic material blends the two into fertile, permeable soil.

Compost, leaf mold, and peat moss are organic or humus-making materials. Peat moss, readily available at plant counters, is the one most of us rely on to make a satisfactory potting soil.

Fir bark ground in ¼- to 1-inch particles is often used for potting orchids and other epiphytic plants, bromeliads, and some gesneriads such as columneas.

Other materials often added to potting mixtures are horticultural grade expanded mica (one trade name is Vermiculite, so prevalent that it is used as a common noun), sphagnum moss, and pebble-size horticultural-grade perlite, which most plant hobbyists refer to as sponge rock, although there is a trademarked product made of perlite which is named Sponge Rok.

Vermiculite, sphagnum moss, and perlite make good additions to potting soil or they can be used alone or in combination to propagate plants. With added nutrients they can be used for growing plants too. Generally when I am mixing potting soils, I feel free to substitute vermiculite for leaf mold (both make the soil spongy and help keep it well aerated), and perlite for sand (perlite is feather-light, and more easily carried around the home and garden than sand).

The addition of ground charcoal to potting soil makes it more porous and keeps it fresh, or "sweet" as our grandmothers might have said.

Potting Mixtures

Average garden soil is seldom used for potting plants, but it can be used as a part of a potting mixture. If your garden has had liberal applications of compost, manure, or leaf mold, you can use garden soil in larger proportions, say as half of a potting mixture.

Plant counters and nurseries carry large lines of ready-mixed potting soils for green or flowering plants as well as cacti and other succulents. The one commercially available material with which I have had complete success is Black Magic Planter Mix and this same firm's African Violet Mix. If I lived in New England, I would probably purchase all of my potting soil and propagating medium from the greenhouses of Albert Buell, Eastford, Connecticut. However, distance is too great to ship his marvelous growing mediums for use in my lighted gardens. It may be that there is an outstanding grower in your area, however, who makes his personal potting soil available. If so, give it a try.

Soil recipes are legion, many of them tailored to fit the requirements of hobby plants such as African violets, begonias, fuchsias, gloxinias, and orchids. If the mixture you are using grows thrifty, blooming plants, continue using it. If you want to experiment with a new mixture, start out with one or two plants, never the entire lot of them. A basic mixture suitable for most plants, with the exception of some cacti and other succulents, bromeliads, and, perhaps, geraniums, can be made of equal parts garden loam, sand (or perlite), and peat moss. For humus-loving plants such as rex begonias, I recommend this basic mixture with the addition of one part well-rotted leaf mold; and, if I do not have the leaf mold, then I substitute one part of vermiculite.

Mixtures tailored to suit the needs of specific plants are given in the chapters describing these plants.

The John Innes soil mixture, long a favorite with English gardeners, can be used as a potting mixture for all plants for which the peat moss, sand, and garden-loam mixture is advised. This mixture is more difficult to assemble, but results may justify the added work.

Prepare a base of:

2 parts hoof and horn meal
2 parts superphosphate
1 part sulfate of potash

Add three-fourths ounce of gypsum to one-fourth pound of this base to one bushel of the following soil mixture:

2 parts sand
3 parts peat moss
7 parts loam

Soil specialists at Cornell University have evolved an artificial mixture which also works well for growing most plants. This is called Peat-Lite:

4 quarts #2 grade vermiculite
4 quarts shredded peat moss
1 tablespoonful (level) powdered 20 per cent superphosphate
2 tablespoons ground limestone

Plus your choice of *one* of the following (but not both):

1½ tablespoons 33 per cent ammonium nitrate
OR
4 tablespoons 5-10-5 fertilizer

Soil Sterilization

Potting soil should be sterilized or pasteurized to destroy harmful bacteria. One of the easiest ways to do this is to put the soil in a pan, add a cup of water to each gallon of mixture, center a small potato in the soil, set the oven regulator at 180 degrees F., and bake the soil until the potato is done. Cool the soil at least twenty-four hours before using.

There are several chemical sterilants on the market, some of which are capsules to be inserted in the soil according to manufacturer's directions. Soilfume Caps are an example of this kind of product. Formaldehyde, too, is a chemical sterilant. To sterilize a half bushel of soil, mix 1¼ tablespoons of formaldehyde in a cup of water and pour over the top of the soil. Cover for twenty-four hours with a sheet of heavy polyethylene plastic, then remove the plastic and air the soil.

Many growers kill some soil-borne bacteria in small amounts of soil by pouring through the soil a kettle of boiling water, and using the soil when it has cooled. This method doesn't begin to be as effective as heating in the oven (or in a covered barbecue unit used in your garage or outdoors) or chemical sterilization; it may be used, however, as a substitute.

Soilless Culture

It is entirely possible to raise ornamental plants and vegetables by soilless or hydroponic culture. With this method, material such as excelsior or wood shavings is used to hold the plants. I have experimented with only one form of this culture, using a soluble fertilizer (Cangro) developed especially for this type of growing. I found it highly successful with miniature roses, begonias, ornamental peppers, and Jerusalem cherries. No doubt it could be adapted to most houseplants. A friend in Florida uses it for dozens of different plants growing in her lath house.

Select a can of suitable size for the plants you want to grow. Halfway up the can cut several holes entirely around the can. Soak shavings (not sawdust) in a solution of nutrients made by adding a teaspoonful of Cangro to a gallon of water. Fill can to the top with shavings. Use plants that have been growing in sphagnum moss or vermiculite, or bare-root plants such as roses for your first venture. Poke a hole in the shavings, insert the plant to the level of the lower leaves. If the can is pint size, sprinkle one-fourth teaspoonful of the dry nutrient mixture on top of the shavings. Water until the lower half of the can is filled with solution. Keep shavings moist by wetting as often as necessary with a solution of one teaspoonful of nutrient mixture to one gallon of water.

Caution: Don't try this method of soilless culture in decorative cabinets or lamps, because the water sometimes flows out of the holes, spotting furniture, even though you may have the can settled in a saucer.

Although my experience with soilless culture has been with Cangro, the more widely available Hyponex is outstanding for this purpose. It may be purchased at local garden centers, plant counters, and by mail from many firms.

Your Choice of Containers

Containers need not be utilitarian, though the familiar clay pot still remains high on the list of favorite plant containers. Plastic pots in a wide variety of shapes and colors are available and are suitable for culture of every kind of plant. Plants growing in clay pots dry out faster than those growing in plastic or glazed pots.

There are special containers too for diverse uses. One that

is well suited to African violet growth and display comes
in three parts: a plastic saucer filled with a sponge; a wide,
open-bottomed jardiniere, which sits on the saucer; and a
clear plastic rim which tops the jardiniere. This rim holds
leaves out in pretty, symmetrical formation. Plants growing
in 4-inch clay pots can be settled comfortably in this fancy
container.

You can make your own jardinieres (a container large
enough to act as a receptacle for a potted plant) from handsome metal vessels or china crockery. Before putting a
potted plant in this type of jardiniere, add a layer of pebbles to the bottom of the jardiniere.

You can make all manner of pretty pots from white ele-
phants you may find among your dishes—a soup tureen that
no longer matches or contrasts well with other dishes, mugs,
jugs, cups or what-have-you. Before planting in containers
minus drainage holes, add a generous layer of pot chips and
crushed charcoal. Plants in these containers seldom need
watering as often as other plants and there is the ever-
present danger of overwatering such plantings.

Strawberry jars, a type of pot with several openings
around the sides, make an excellent display area for small
African violets, miniature or slow-growing vines such as
Helxine soleirolii (baby's-tears), cacti, and other succulents,
episcias and many other plants. Some of the red-clay strawberry jars have drainage holes in them, but glazed and plastic ones may not. Here, too, an extra helping of bottom
drainage material is needed. Add to the welfare of such
plantings by centering in the container a moss stick or tube
of chicken wire filled with sphagnum moss. Water over the
stick or down the tube. A new plastic jar on the market has
built-in water well with small openings to let moisture seep
into the soil.

Before planting a wire- or wooden-slatted hanging basket
or box, line it with green sheet moss or unmilled sphagnum,
then fill with soil.

Containers of pressed peat or bagasse, a residue remaining from sugar cane, make excellent starter pots. Seed can be planted directly in them or they can be used for transplanting seedlings. Plants need not be removed from these pots before transferring them to soil. Plant the pot and plant in the new pot of soil or into the open ground of a garden. Roots penetrate these peat or bagasse pots, moving into the fresh soil with no setback in growth.

My personal preference for container gardens under lights is found in the uniformity and immaculate appearance of all white plastic pots in varying sizes. Combined with the white reflectors and white walls around my fluorescent-lighted gardens, these white pots add to the pleasant brightness and provide a perfect foil for foliage and flowers.

There are several plastic trays available for holding plant collections. Tube Craft of Cleveland, for example, manufactures an excellent line that is easily obtainable by mail. You can also have a local tinner make rustproof trays to fit growing areas of all sizes. Pot saucers are available in clay, plastic, and ceramic materials too.

Potting and Repotting

Pot or repot plants into clean pots. Scrub away accumulated fertilizer salts, which leave a whitish residue on the pot. Use hot, sudsy detergent water and a stiff brush to remove soil and algae. Soak new clay pots for a few hours before using them. If you like a plant enough to consider it for your garden, get it set for a long and successful growing life by potting properly.

Small African violets, begonias, vines, and other green plants are purchased in 2¼-inch pots. Likely these small pots are filled with roots and the plants are ready for a shift into 3-inch pots. A general rule about potting runs something like this: It's better to under-pot than over-pot a plant.

Shift plants to pots one size larger than the ones they were growing in.

This is sage advice unless the plant you contemplate transplanting has grown in a greenhouse or a pebble-filled tray where roots grew out the bottom the pot and stretched into the freedom of the moist bench medium. Judge the size of the pot for these top-heavy plants by measuring the height of the plant. Transplant it to a pot with a rim measuring one-third to one-half the height of the plant. For instance, a 15-inch rubber plant (*Ficus elastica*) growing in a 3-inch pot might well be transplanted directly to a 5-inch container, skipping the 4-incher.

Transplanting or repotting is needed whenever the pot becomes filled with roots. The kind of plant, its age, and the season are factors determining how often to transplant. Check rootballs by removing from the pot. Do this by straddling the base of the stem with two fingers pressed firmly into the soil. Tap the edge of the pot on a solid object—table, counter, or piece of wood—and the pot should slide off easily. If the roots fill the soil, showing outside the top and bottom, it's time to transplant. If the bottom of the soil crumbles away from the rootball, add some more soil to the pot and repot in the original container.

Some plants such as gloxinia and amaryllis can be cultivated for many years in the same pot. However, a change of soil is usually indicated annually, and that is done when the tubers or bulbs have finished their dormant period and begun to show growth. Some growers change the soil on amaryllis only every second year, adding a layer of fresh topsoil only in the intervening year.

When you pot a plant you actually begin from the bottom up, for the first step in planting into any type of container lies in adding some drainage to the bottom of the pot. If the pot has a drainage hole, place a broken piece of clay pot over it, concave side down. This enables water to drain from the pot, yet keeps the soil from sliding out with it. Add a shallow layer of pebbles, gravel, sponge rock, or any of the three plus some broken charcoal. The charcoal isn't necessary, but it aids in keeping soil desirably fresh. If the container is larger than 6 inches in diameter, add a layer of sphagnum moss too.

Now you are ready to add soil and set the plant. Hold the plant in the center of the pot and spoon soil around the roots. Firm the roots into the soil with your fingertips, working carefully so you don't break fine feeder roots. And don't forget to leave room at the top for watering—a half inch for pots to 4 inches in diameter, an inch or more for larger ones. After potting, tap the base of the pot on a firm surface to settle the soil.

Water the new planting thoroughly by setting in a pan or saucer of water and letting it soak up enough water so the soil surface looks and feels damp.

Peat moss is difficult to moisten and many growers moisten mixtures containing peat moss a day or two ahead of actual potting.

Label, Lest You Forget

I like to label my plants. Even if I did not have a large collection, I think it would be a good idea. You might not need to know the name of a plant, but it is nice to know the date you planted it, where you purchased it, or the name of the person who gave it to you.

As your collection progresses, it is well to learn the correct names of your plants. Even Latin names will become as familiar as your next door neighbor's if you mention them often in conversation.

7

Plant Propagation under Fluorescent Lights

The day you begin to propagate plants in a fluorescent-lighted garden you will have entered a new and engrossing world. Miracles will happen every day . . . sprouting seeds, rooting cuttings, bursting seedpods on plants you hybridized, and first blooms on your own seedlings. The process of producing new plants under lights, just as with natural light, can be divided into two groups: asexual or vegetative, and sexual or seed. Asexual plant multiplication entails the use of cuttings or slips, divisions, offsets, air-layers, or grafts. Sexual propagation makes use of seeds and spores—purchased or homegrown.

All methods of vegetative reproduction can be carried out under fluorescent setups having 20 to 74 watts of illumination or more, fourteen to sixteen hours daily. Plant parts root more rapidly when placed in a closed container such as a covered terrarium, a plastic- or glass-covered container of clear glass or plastic found in a kitchen—refrigerator dishes, bread boxes, casseroles, or cheese boxes. (Heat a pointed instrument such as a nut or ice pick and make ventilation and drainage holes in tops and bottoms of plastic containers.) If beads of moisture appear inside the cover, remove it, wipe dry, then replace.

If you want to propagate a single leaf or cutting you can

give it a humid atmosphere by slipping a drinking glass or a plastic Baggie over it. African violets often root in two or three weeks.

If you propagate plants in a cool room, say below 68 degrees, use an electric soil-heating cable to raise the soil temperature to about 72 degrees. This gentle bottom heat encourages rapid rooting.

Propagating boxes and pots of sun-loving plants such as cacti and other succulents, geraniums, and many hardwood or softwood cuttings should be placed about 6 inches from the lights. They'll root farther from the lights, but the cuttings grow during this time and if they are not receiving enough light they will become spindly.

Cuttings and divisions of African violets, other gesneriads, begonias, and low-light plants such as ivy, philodendron, and other foliage plants grow roots readily at 11 or more inches from the tubes.

Selecting a Propagating Medium

Propagate plants in milled sphagnum moss, vermiculite, horticultural-grade perlite (sponge rock), sand, peat moss, or in a mixture of two or more of these. Bagasse, a cinderlike residue from sugar-cane mills, is being used today by some persons for rooting cuttings. If you have only a leaf or two, root in water.

Milled sphagnum moss, vermiculite, or perlite taken directly from the container need not be sterilized. However, if you have dipped into it with pots or labels used on other plants, better sterilize or pasteurize it. Sand and peat moss should also be sterilized. Sieve peat moss when you are using it for growing fine seeds. I like to add a layer of charcoal to all propagation boxes. It keeps the media sweet and clean.

Vegetative Propagation

African violets, some begonias, gloxinias, philodendron, sedum, kalanchoe, and peperomia are plants that can be propagated from a single leaf. Other plants such as fuchsia, geranium, and coleus are propagated from terminal shoots or slips taken from the top or branches.

A warm, humid atmosphere is necessary for satisfactory rooting. Cuttings growing in glass- or plastic-covered boxes placed under lights in a 70- to 75-degree room root readily.

One of my favorite propagators is a large, transparent plastic box, 8 inches deep, 12 inches wide, and 16 inches long. This type is sold by plantsmen. You may also be able to obtain a case of this kind from a department store. (Many people use them for storing sweaters and other woolen garments.) Even the round, clear, plastic hatboxes make good propagation cases, though they take up more space than the straight-sided, right-angled ones.

Use a sharp knife to take cuttings. African violets handle easiest when they have about an inch of petiole (leaf stem). (They will root with no petiole at all, too.) It is usually a good practice to dip the ends of cuttings in a hormone powder such as Rootone, although it pays to go easy; geraniums, for example, may be damaged by rooting hormones. Insert the cutting firmly into the moistened propagating medium. Label the cutting with varietal name and planting date.

Taking cuttings from favorite plants is one way to assure additional plants of the same variety. There are a few exceptions: African violets for instance, taken with no petiole may "sport" or mutate, likewise some variegated cuttings may produce only green-leaved plants.

African violet leaves grow larger while being propagated. Gloxinia leaves may wither when they have formed a tuber.

But it won't be long before the small tuber will be showing sprouts.

Tip cuttings of begonias, geraniums, and impatiens taken with buds on them often bloom in the propagating case. Strip enough leaves from these cuttings so no leaves are buried in the propagating medium.

If propagation is new to you, it's fun to watch roots form in a glass or bottle of water. Use colored glass and it won't collect algae. Roots form rapidly, sometimes in two or three days on coleus. When the root crop seems fairly heavy, transplant the cutting to a small pot of sphagnum moss or your usual potting soil. Water-rooted cuttings grow more succulent roots than those rooted in other media. When water-rooted cuttings are transplanted to soil they often take quite a setback.

Gloxinias and rex begonias can also be propagated by making slits on the back of the heavy leaf veins, then placing the leaf with its underside to the propagating material. You may have to peg it down with wooden toothpicks or small stones. New plants arise from the cut areas. Rex begonias can also be propagated from wedge-shaped cuttings containing a section of the heavy vein.

Cacti and other succulent cuttings should dry out before inserting them in the rooting medium. The drying period may be twenty-four hours or a week, depending on the weather (it takes longer if damp) and the age of the plant (large cuttings from older plants need a longer drying time).

Many growers still let geranium cuttings dry overnight or for a few hours before striking them in the medium, but most commercial growers and advanced hobbyists advise stripping off a pair of the lower leaves and planting them immediately.

Mallet cuttings are often used to propagate philodendron, rare geraniums, chrysanthemums, ivy and rubber plants (*Ficus elastica*). Cut the leaves with a growing bud in the

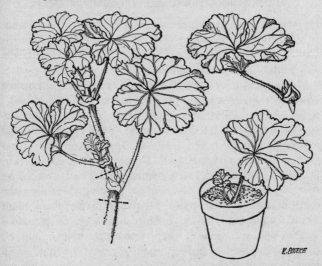

Figure 2. Mallet cutting of common geranium. Upper right, the cutting is ready for insertion into moist sand or vermiculite. Lower right, the cutting has rooted and a new plant is sprouting from the leaf axil.

leaf axil, leaving about a half to 1 inch of stem above and below the leaf node. The leaf is the handle, the stem the head of what appears to be a small mallet. Insert such cuttings with the bud pointing upward.

To propagate sansevierias, make 1- to 3-inch sections of leaves. Cut them horizontally and insert in a rooting medium. Leaf sections of the variegated *Sansevieria trifasciata laurenti* have always given me new plants of plain green, but recently a reader of *Park's Floral Magazine* wrote in disagreement, saying that variegated leaf cuttings produced like plants for her. At least, in my experience, I still say that if you want more identical plants, divide the old sansevieria at the base.

Some foliage plants such as alocasias, dieffenbachias, dracaenas, philodendrons, and Chinese evergreens can be reproduced through 4-inch stem cuttings. Dip the cuttings in sulfur or Fermate to prevent rot. Lay the cuttings on the rooting medium in a closed propagation case. Plants develop from the eyes, which are undeveloped buds.

Plants with stolons or runners such as strawberry-begonia (*Saxifraga sarmentosa*), episcias (African violet relatives), some African violets, and spider plant (*Chlorophytum elatum*) can be propagated by severing these new growths and rooting in any preferred medium. The walking iris (*Neomarica northiana*) sends forth flowers on long blades. The flowers are followed by new plants which can be rooted by severing from the old plant or by pegging them into the earth near the mother plant. Piggyback or pickaback plant (*Tolmiea menziesi*) bears young plants on top of its mature leaves. To have more of these interesting plants, snip off some of the plantlets and root them any way you think you'll have the most pleasure, for these are indeed sturdy plants.

African violets, gloxinias, and other gesneriads, fibrous-rooted begonias, bromeliads, many cacti and other succulents, grow new plants as offsets or suckers at the base of the plant. These small plants should be severed with a sharp knife and rooted as cuttings. A coating of hormone powder hastens root formation.

Amaryllis, fisherman's net (*Bowiea volubilis*), some haemanthus, zephyranthes, and many other bulbous plants increase by producing new bulbs or offsets. Remove these when they are about two years old and transplant to single pots of soil. Many small bulblets cling to a mature bulb of the sea-onion (*Urginea maritima*). You can shuck them off as easily as peas from a pod and they'll root in any medium other than water. In my greenhouse they often fall from the mother bulb and root themselves as they lie on the surface of moist vermiculite in the bench.

Plants with more than one stem or crown can be divided by severing the additional stems and rooting them. A twelve-year-old clivia I have is past ready for division. It shows 15 well-developed plants in a 20-inch tub. Cane-stemmed begonias and African violets also grow additional plants. You can divide these by severing the new plants and some roots with a knife or by knocking the plant from its pot and separating the plants. Dust cut parts with sulfur or Fermate. Plant divisions in sterilized soil. In the case of tender plants such as violets and begonias, it's well to slip a transparent plastic bag over the planting to hasten the adjusting period.

Grafting Houseplants

Plants can also be propagated by grafting. The indoor gardener will have fun trying to graft miniature roses, geraniums, and cacti.

Choose a potted plant which will be called the standard or *stock*. The *scion*, a budded twig, is shaped and inserted into the growing wood of the stock. The *cambium* (growing bark tissue) on both stock and scion must meet. The scion is fastened to the stock with tape, grafting wax, rubber bands, or in the case of cactus, with cactus needles.

You can produce several kinds of blooms on a single geranium or rose by taking twigs and grafting them onto a single stock.

The Christmas cactus is an easy one to experiment with. Use pereskia, the woody cactus, as a stock. Cut a V-shaped cleft in its center. Trim the scion of Christmas cactus to fit the cleft. Hold together with long cactus spines (never metal pins), or rubber bands. Water sparingly and the scion may show growth within a few months. You can place grafted plants directly under lights, but they must be shaded from sunshine for a few days.

In addition to propagating your houseplants, you can also reproduce favorite shrubby plants for containers and outdoor gardens.

Rooting Cuttings under Lights for Outdoors

Softwood cuttings are made from growing shrubs or trees and are taken in the summer. Hardwood cuttings are made when growth has stopped and plant stems have become woody. I've found it best to take hardwood cuttings in late fall, after the leaves have fallen.

Most of these cuttings will root in daytime temperatures to 75 degrees, with a 10-degree drop at night.

Acacia, abutilon (flowering maple), aralia, *Araucaria excelsa* (Norfolk Island pine), ardisia, blueberries, gardenias, peaches, and roses are but a few of the softwood cuttings you'll enjoy propagating under lights. Roses will root and bud under lights in six months. Either softwood or hardwood cuttings can be used.

Azaleas (rhododendron), boxwood, conifers, and grapes are among the hardwood cuttings that root easily under lights.

Softwood cuttings should be about 4 inches long, each having at least two leaf nodes. Remove the lower pair of leaves. Dip the end of the cutting in hormone powder. Make a planting hole with a small stick or pencil, insert the cutting carefully so the powder doesn't rub off. Plant cuttings so one node is below the surface, the other above the surface. Firm the medium about the stems.

The process for rooting hardwood cuttings is the same except there may be some hardwood cuttings such as grapes that will be minus all leaves.

Rooting time varies from one to four months. When plants are well rooted, transplant them to pots and grow in a cool, lighted area or in the outdoor garden.

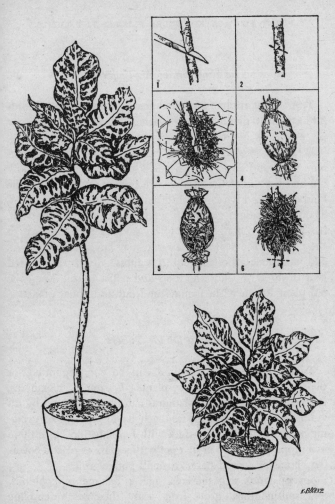

Figure 3. Air-layering an ungainly plant of hybrid croton: (1) Notch stem with sharp knife or razor blade. (2) Insert piece of toothpick to hold cut place open. (3) Surround with moist sphagnum moss. (4) Cover with polyethylene plastic; tie at top and bottom. (5) Roots can be seen as they start to form; be sure moss never dries out. (6) When root growth is vigorous, sever from old stem at dotted line. Repot in container of suitable size.

The Fine Art of Air-Layering

Turn leggy rubber plants, dracaenas, and similar plants into compact plants by air-layering. To do this remove a piece of bark below a node, or cut a notch in the stem.

Wrap the smooth or cut area with a fistful of damp sphagnum moss and cover it with polyethylene plastic. Seal both top and bottom of the plastic with tape or Twistems, or the kind of covered wires which often come with freezer boxes. The moss inside a good seal will stay moist until the stem has produced enough roots to be severed from the rest of the plant. If the seal leaks air you may have to open it and add additional moisture to the moss. Sever the rooted growth directly below the roots and pot it in soil. Keep the old plant if you wish; it may send out additional plants.

How to Divide Tubers

Tubers, bulbs, and rhizomes can be cut, separated, or divided to produce more plants. Gloxinias, gloxineras, tuberous begonias, and caladiums can be propagated by dividing the tubers into pieces, each having an eye or growing point. Coat the cut surface with Fermate and place them in a propagation case or in a pot with a glass or plastic covering. Transfer rooted parts to small pots of soil.

Several kinds of gesneriads, such as achimenes, kohlerias, and smithianthas, grow from scaly rhizomes resembling small pine cones. Rhizomes can be broken in two, or scales can be separated and planted individually as seeds. Scatter the individual scales on top of moistened propagating medium, cover lightly with more mixture, and they'll soon sprout.

Propagating amaryllis, hyacinths, and lilies through scales

is a tricky business, but you will have fun trying. Choose for your first efforts an easily replaced bulb. In fact, you might start on an onion to familiarize yourself with the procedure. Remove a scale of the bulb with some of the basal tissue intact. Coat the cut area with Fermate, and place the scale in a propagator, basal end inserted into the medium. Little bulbs form around the basal tissue. You can also notch bulbs by making V-shaped marks in the basal tissue; again, coat the cuts with Fermate. Plant the bulb and you will have several small bulbs springing from the cut areas.

Houseplants from Seed

Growing any plant from seed to maturity gives the gardener special pride, but flowering houseplants grown from seed give an amazing amount of pleasure and satisfaction.

You can purchase houseplant seeds from specialists or you can make your plants produce seed. Or, if you want to start a quick and easy way, grow a group of African violets, begonias, gloxinias, or cacti from preseeded planters. These planters have full instructions with them.

Any of the propagation cases suggested for starting plant parts will be fine for growing seed. Plastic- or glass-covered containers are best for they keep the seeds from drying out.

Sprinkle fine seeds such as African violets, other gesneriads, begonias, and similar plants on top of moist milled sphagnum or vermiculite. Do not cover fine seed with additional medium. I find it best to moisten the medium before planting so the seed won't float. Place plantings under the lights, or if the room is cool, set the planting atop a light where it receives some bottom heat from the light tubes. You seldom have to water seeds again before germination, but if you do, mist them with an atomizer or add water with a spoon. Germination time varies with different plants and with the age of the seed. Fresh begonia seed usually germinate in ten to fourteen days. Most plants, except some hardwood types and some bulbous ones, bloom as quickly from seed as from cuttings.

When germination shows, place the planting about 4 inches from the lights. Transplant to individual pots or community pots (several plants to a pot) as soon as you can handle them. Most people transplant when there are four good leaves or seedlings are about the size of a penny.

Press larger seeds such as amaryllis, miniature roses, and geraniums into the soil and cover with about one-fourth inch of mixture.

Hybridize Your Own Varieties under Lights

Make your plants produce their own seed by transferring some pollen from the yellow anthers in the center of a flower to the pistil (elongated object) directly in the middle of the flower. If the pollination is successful the petals soon drop. Label your cross with some kind of small, paper tag. Include this information: Name of seed parent (the one receiving the pollen); name of pollen parent; date of cross. And for future records, write this information in a notebook.

African violets ripen seeds in four to nine months; but amaryllis, gloxinias, and begonias often ripen seed in four to six weeks.

When the seed is ripe the pod shrivels. African violet seedpods become soft and mushy before they start to dry. Clip the ripe seedpod, store it in a labeled envelope or bottle until you are ready to sow.

Species plants such as *Saintpaulia grotei* and *Sinningia pusilla,* pollinated with pollen from the same plant or from another of the same species, produce plants just like themselves. Hybrids such as the named varieties do not come true from seed. You'll get a wide variety of plants from crossings made between flowers on the same plant. When you use pollen from a variety which differs greatly from the seed parent the variety in the seedlings will be even greater. Of course you know not to go too far with these differences. You may cross two African violets that are as different as possible, but you cannot cross an African violet with a pumpkin, for example. Generally it is possible only to cross plants of the same genera, although occasionally we hear of bigeneric crosses, as described in this book in the discussion of gloxineras (see Index).

Trees and Shrubs from Seeds under Lights

To grow your own trees and shrubs from seeds in a fluorescent-lighted garden you will need only bulb pans or pots filled with a moistened mixture of equal parts peat moss and sand, and plastic bags in which to place the pots after the seeds have been sown. In addition, there is an important intangible you will need: lots of patience.

Aside from the pleasure a gardener derives from starting seeds of favorite or rare trees and shrubs, there are practical reasons. If you want trees and shrubs for container gardening, this is a good way to begin. If you want to practice the oriental art of bonsai, seedlings will give you plenty of material with which to work. And to evidence your faith in the future, plant a walnut. It will provide a century of good climbing for children, and generations to come will enjoy the nuts.

The growing of trees and shrubs from seeds is filled with many unknowns. Probably in no other line of plant propagation will you encounter more of nature's tricks. For example, there are some "two-year" seeds. That is, they mature one year, but germination will not occur for at least a year afterward. Types that may behave like this include dogwood, cotoneaster, hawthorne, and some roses.

Some tree and shrub seeds have such a hard coating that

it needs to be nicked with a file before planting, or better, pour boiling water over the seeds, let stand overnight, then drain and plant. Kinds to give this treatment include acacia, albizzia, boxwood, camellia, cercis, honeylocust, juniperus, redbud, and silk tree.

A great majority of tree and shrub seeds need a period of coldness, near freezing, followed by warmth, in order to break dormancy. The natural way to start these seeds is to sow them outdoors in a coldframe in autumn, or into winter if the weather permits. When warm-up comes in the spring, germination begins. You can simulate this period of coolness by a process called "stratification." To do this, mix the seeds with moist sand and peat moss in a Mason jar or plastic container and place in your refrigerator or in a temperature range of approximately 33 to 41 degrees F. for the specified period of time. Then remove and sow.

A four-month stratification period is recommended for buckeye, butternut, Eastern redcedar (*Juniperus virginiana*), hickory, *Magnolia grandiflora*, and black walnut.

Some seeds need to be stratified only two or three months. These include apple, alder, ash, beech, birch, baldcypress, cotoneaster, crab apple, elm, fir, flowering cherry, franklinia, ginkgo, goldenrain tree, hackberry, hawthorne, hemlock, holly, lagerstroemia, ligustrum, lilac, linden, Pacific madrone (*Arbutus menziesii*), maple, nandina, oak, peach, pear, persimmon, pine, poplar, pyracantha, quince, redwood, Russian olive, spruce, sweet gum, tulip-tree, black tupelo, and yew.

Still another group requires only a two-month period of storage at 33 to 41 degrees before being sown in a warm place for germination. Kinds include cupressus, Jack pine (*Pinus banksiana*), longleaf pine (*P. palustris*), pitch pine (*P. rigida*), shortleaf pine (*P. echinata*), and American sycamore.

Another group requires first a period of two to four months at 68 to 80 degrees F., then a period of two to four months

Rex begonia leaves, whole or sections with main veins included, root readily under lights in a humidity-preserving terrarium like this. Three containers at left show leaves rooted in water; at right older cuttings rooted this way have been transplanted to pots of growing medium and evidence lusty clusters of new plants. (BRILMAYER)

This bookcase with glass doors was rescued from second-hand furniture store and converted to a lighted plant propagator. (BRILMAYER)

Author's double-decker lighted garden in attic room provides 16 square feet of growing space for African violets, seedlings of many tropicals, miniature garden in brandy snifter, episcias, nautilocalyx, gloxinias, *Exacum affine*, and miniature roses. (BRILMAYER)

Bubble bowls, brandy snifters, antique bottles, dish gardens, and other similar terrariums thrive in lighted gardens. (SELECT STUDIOS)

Bottle garden landscape for under-light culture includes English ivy with gold-flecked leaves, aucuba (gold-dust plant), African violet, and carpeting of baby's-tears. (OWENS-ILLINOIS)

Basement garden of African violets in home of Lizeta Tenney Hamilton, Oradell, New Jersey. Note tremendous number of flowers and luxuriant foliage. (FRIEDMAN-ABELES, COURTESY SYLVANIA)

Effects of too much light on a pink-flowered African violet. Too much red light causes the rough, bubbly appearance. Smoother green leaves show how plants recuperate when moved away from the lights, or when the number of light hours is decreased. (SELECT STUDIOS)

Tigrina hybrid gloxinia from Antonelli Brothers would make an excitin subject for any lighted garden. (VESTER DICK)

New small-growing gloxinia slip-per from Fischer Greenhouses is called 'Red Flicker.'

at 33 to 41 degrees, followed by warmth, for germination. Give this treatment to Rocky Mountain juniper (*Juniperus scopulorum*), Western juniper (*J. occidentalis*), silverbell, and fringe-tree (chionanthus).

Seeds that are surrounded by a pulp need first to have this removed. To do so, soak them in water until the fleshy covering becomes soft; then wash it off, drain, and air-dry the seeds before sowing. Kinds that need this treatment include barberry, holly, magnolia, pyracantha, rose, and viburnum.

Willow, poplar, and some maple seeds are short-lived and need to be planted soon after harvest. White-alder, catalpa, citrus, photinia, podocarpus, sourwood, and viburnum also do well when sown as soon as ripe. If oak or chestnut become thoroughly air-dried, they need stratification in order to break dormancy. Camellia seeds ripen from late summer to early fall, depending on climate and variety, and the sooner they are sown afterward, the better.

There are several strains of outstanding azalea hybrids available in seed form. These include Kaempferi, Exbury, Kurume, and Mollis hybrids, and a blend called simply "Hardy." These seeds are small and need to be merely dusted across the surface of moist peat moss and sand, then given a scant covering of milled sphagnum moss. In a temperature range of 60 to 70 degrees, germination occurs in fourteen to twenty-one days. The seedlings are tiny, but when true leaves have developed they should be transplanted about 1 × 1 inch apart in a flat or community pot. Later they may be placed in individual containers, or lined out in a nursery bed that is well protected.

If you are in doubt about how to start a packet of rare tree or shrub seeds, divide it. Sow half just as you would any common seeds such as marigolds. Stratify the other half for two to four months, then sow them as you did the others.

Whenever you are ready to plant tree and shrub seeds, either immediately following harvest, after stratification, or after the pulp has been removed and they are dry again, select bulb pans or standard pots of convenient size and fill them with a moist mixture of equal parts peat moss and sand. Cover small seeds to the depth of their own thickness; large ones to twice this amount. Press the surface with the palm of your hand. Set the pots in a basin of water until beads of moisture show at the surface. Remove and allow to drain. Then place inside a plastic bag and position beneath fluorescent lights (about 6 inches below two 40-watt tubes burned fourteen to sixteen hours out of every twenty-four). Watch for signs of germination. When you see a seedling, remove the plastic. Be sure the growing medium never dries out.

If seedlings crowd, transplant to community pots, flats, or individual containers. Seedlings that are small enough to be left in the peat and sand mixture for more than a few weeks will need to be fed about once a month with liquid house-plant fertilizer. Pots and flats of tree and shrub seedlings can be summered outdoors in a protected place. Be sure the growing medium is kept evenly moist at all times, and this may mean twice-daily watering in summer. Seedlings of hardy trees and shrubs may be wintered over in a cold-frame, and transplanted to nursery rows for growing on the second spring.

8

Coping with the Inevitable: Pests, Diseases, and Problems

Good culture prevents most plant troubles in under-light gardens, but you need to be able to recognize and cope with various common problems. Make it your number one rule to isolate newly purchased plants for at least ten days so that any pest they may harbor can be detected before possible spread to healthy plants already in your collection. Even if you cannot determine a specific pest or disease, don't put the plant with others unless it is in radiant good health.

Impeccable housekeeping in your plant room, and this means for one pot or a thousand, is another deterrent to all kinds of problems. Keep withering leaves picked up and removed. Don't let them accumulate on the soil surface or in the bench. Likewise with faded flowers; remove them promptly, and if petals shatter, as those of geraniums, take that little extra trouble needed to pick up every petal from the foliage, the soil, and the bench.

Several times a year, at least once a quarter, I make it a practice to go through my entire collection of potted plants, taking time to pick up every pot. I inspect the plant from above and from below so that any signs of pest infestation (especially those that collect on leaf undersides) can be detected. I use a stiff brush to remove any fertilizer salts that may have collected on the pot rim, and then a soft cloth is used to wipe the pot clean before it is returned to the bench. At least once a year all moisture-holding material used in the benches is removed, added to my compost pile, and replaced with either perlite or vermiculite. Both are light in weight and inexpensive, quickly and easily added to the benches.

Another preventive measure is the weekly application of a houseplant pesticide applied by means of a convenient aerosol. If one of these is kept handy, you can develop the habit of catching pest infestations before they have a chance to spread. In nearly twenty years of under-light gardening, I have never had to cope with a really serious problem of pest or disease. As a home greenhouse gardener, there have been a few times when a hose-end sprayer has been put to use, and to be really thorough I have had to resort to individual dipping of plants (this to thwart an infestation of mealybugs that got out of hand).

A reading glass is a helpful aid in spotting small insects such as aphids, thrips, and white flies, but you will need a pocket microscope to really see cyclamen mites, red spider mites, and nematodes. Slugs, mealybugs, and scale are readily seen with the naked eye.

No matter how proficient you become in identifying plant pests, there is no substitute for good culture. This includes light, temperature, and humidity in the right combination with a suitable growing medium, properly moistened and fertilized. If you have a plant that is not growing well, and it has no apparent insect or disease, research the environment it needs. If you cannot find specific instructions in this book, or in other volumes to which you have access, try to determine the conditions under which the plant would grow in its native habitat, then attempt to duplicate them in your under-light garden.

Plant Pests to Know

Aphids are the soft-bodied little plant lice that cluster on new growth. There are many kinds, but only a pale-green type has ever infested my under-light plants. Eradication is simple with an aerosol pesticide. For a severe infestation, spray or dip in malathion (mix 1 teaspoon malathion emulsion to each gallon of water).

Cyclamen mites are a serious enemy of under-light gardens, especially with African violets, since the damage they cause is so similar to that caused by unbalanced light conditions (leaving lights on continuously around the clock). These mites are less than ⅓₂ inch long. First signs of attack may be seen in malformed tip growth (the young center leaves in the rosette of an African violet), and in distorted flower stalks, buds, and streaked petals. An African violet with a severe attack of cyclamen mites will show thickly furred new leaves. The safest treatment is to dip the plants at weekly intervals in a solution made by mixing 1 teaspoon kelthane emulsion to each gallon of water. Repeat at weekly intervals until plant growth is normal. Use of the dangerous systemic, sodium selenate, is advocated by many African violet growers. If you are interested in this means of control, check the catalogs of specialists to find a source (see chapter 22). Current recommendations for use of sodium selenate will be found on the container.

Earthworms are sometimes brought into lighted gardens from plants that have been summered outdoors. These welcome visitors to the compost pile are most unpleasant inside, and I hope that organic gardeners will forgive my suggesting the use of a soil drench made by mixing 1 level teaspoon of 50 per cent wettable chlordane powder in 1 quart of water.

Gnats are the adult form of white maggots that are often present in humusy soil. Gnats themselves are not harmful to plants, but they are not desirable to have in the house. A really severe infestation of the maggots may cause damage to delicate plant roots, and therefore, if you are using soil that contains a large amount of decaying plant material, either pasteurize it first (see chapter 6), or drench with chlordane as suggested for earthworms.

Mealybugs are grayish insects coated with a white wax. They are sap suckers, and if not brought under control rapidly the results can be disastrous. One type attacks leaves, usually on the undersides, in crevices, and leaf axils, as much out of your sight and touch as possible. The other may be described as a white fuzzy ball about an eighth of an inch in diameter that attaches to the roots and drains away the life of the plant. Control for the leaf types is the same as that suggested for aphids; for soil mealybugs, drenching is the answer, using a malathion solution (1 teaspoon malathion emulsion per gallon of water). There is one big difference, however, when you are treating for mealybugs; aphids have a way of running their course and disappearing, but not mealybugs. Deal with them as real culprits. I can't sleep well if I know there is a mealybug around my plants.

Nematodes are microscopic eelworms that live in the roots of plants, and occasionally in leaves. I have experienced them only twice, first in the roots of 'Mme. Salleron,' a favorite small-growing fancy-leaved geranium, and second when I discovered brown, papery areas in the leaves of 'Corallina de Lucerna,' the old-fashioned angel-wing begonia. The geranium showed its symptoms by appearing to stop growing. My first brief examination revealed no signs of black rot, the usual problem with ailing geraniums, so I supposed the plant was taking a rest. After a few more weeks the plant took on an over-all dull appearance, and about this time I removed it from the pot and shook away the soil. There the signs of nematodes at work were obvious: swollen knots all along the roots.

In spite of the advanced knowledge we have today in

pest control, the experts still have no recommendation for eradicating nematodes once a plant becomes infected. The only thing to do is discard the plant, soil, and pot. If you use only sterilized potting soil, nematodes are not likely to attack your plants.

Red spider mites are common everywhere, and thus they are likely to be your problem at one time or another. These are difficult if not impossible to see without a hand lens or pocket microscope, but they leave obvious symptoms: fine webs on leaf undersides and in leaf axils, and yellowing leaves. The kelthane treatment prescribed for cyclamen mites will also work for red spider mites, but their presence also indicates less than ideal growing conditions. Be sure there is ample relative humidity around your plants. Provide free circulation of some fresh air daily. Avoid hot, dry conditions combined with stale air. Sometimes all you need to do with red spider mites is wash infested plants with a strong stream of water, and correct the growing conditions.

Scale in two forms has been troublesome in my plant collection. Many years ago I discovered that an angel-wing begonia with its attractive silver-spotted leaves was also developing tan-colored oblong spots in an irregular pattern on leaf surfaces. Closer inspection revealed that these were on stems and leaf stalks too, and soon I diagnosed a good case of soft brown scale. For a small infestation, these can be removed by flicking them off with the point of a pocket knife. For a severe infestation, dipping in nicotine sulfate (Black Leaf 40) is an effective means of control. In recent years a specimen plant of dwarf orange or calamondin (*Citrus mitis*) was plagued by a hard white, oblong scale. Individual removal of these would also be a means of control, but by the time I noticed them on my large plant, repeated dippings in nicotine sulfate were required. Later I have noticed small infestations trying to make a comeback, but my handy aerosol of houseplant pesticide stops them.

Slugs and snails inhabit dark, damp places where decaying vegetation is present. A vigilant sanitation program is an effective means of control. Picking up every pot and wiping it clean several times yearly is also a help. If these pests gain headway, damaged plant parts, especially tender flower buds and tip growth, will result. If this happens, use one of the commercially available baits that contains metaldehyde.

Sow bugs and pill bugs, known to my children as rolypolies (an absurdly affectionate name, to my way of thinking), are hard-shelled gray pests that live under flowerpots and pieces of wood, feeding on decaying matter. As unpleasant as they are outdoors, they are intolerable inside. Drench the soil as prescribed in this chapter for control of earthworms.

Springtails are the tiny grayish insects that busily dart back and forth over moist soil, and sometimes in the medium used in plant benches. These are similar to the psocids you have probably observed in the pages of old magazines and books kept in a somewhat damp place. Which of the two you may see in your indoor garden doesn't really matter. If you want to be rid of them, drench the soil as described in this chapter for control of earthworms.

Thrips are very slender black insects that suck the sap from flower petals and leaves. Indoors, gloxinias seem to be their preference above all other plants, and outdoors they are most noted for being troublesome to gladiolus. Signs on a gloxinia include rusty leaf undersides and reddish stems. Eventually flower buds will wither and droop, their stalks completely sapped of strength. Use houseplant aerosol.

White flies are small insects that cluster on the undersides of leaves, causing some damage there, but mostly spreading harmful plant diseases, especially troublesome viruses occasionally present in geraniums. The first time you pick up a begonia, fuchsia, geranium, abutilon, or gardenia and these insects fly away in all directions, you will know why I abhor them almost as much as mealybugs. A houseplant pesticide aerosol is about the most effective means of control, since it affords the action needed to get those in the air as well as those that remain on the plant. Repeat at five- to seven-day intervals as necessary.

Systemics for Pest Control

Although the dangerous systemic, sodium selenate, has been used by growers of African violets for several years in the effective control of cyclamen mites and other common pests, there are several new systemics on the market that are not nearly as toxic to human beings. Two that I am presently testing, and which are on the market for home gardens, are Scope (Chemagro Corporation, Kansas City, Missouri), and Systemic Insect Spray (Elanco Products Company, 640 South Alabama Street, Indianapolis 6, Indiana). If you cannot find these at your local garden center, where you can study the container labels to determine current recommendations for pot plants, contact the manufacturers.

9

Decorative Gardens That Save
Time and Space

Decorators use green plants as important appointments in furnishing a room. They select large specimen plants to emphasize a focal point or to obscure an architectural flaw. Plants are chosen in proper relation to the size of the room and the area to be decorated. A grouping of plants gives a dramatic effect that is unattainable with a scattering of small, singly potted plants.

You can achieve this too by filling a corner with a group of 5- or 6-inch pots of dieffenbachia, schefflera, and philodendron, or a planter box filled with these enduring foliage plants. These low-light plants will exist for months without additional light, but they expand beautifully with as little as four hours illumination daily from a 60-watt incandescent bulb burning over them.

Planter boxes are available in all sizes, in plastic, wood, and metal. To maintain plants in these boxes, add at least an inch of drainage material to 12-inch squatty planters, proportionately more to larger ones. Porous soil containing some charcoal is best for planters. Submerge potted plants in the soil or remove the pots and plant directly into the moistened soil. Planter depth is important: 6 inches is the minimum, 12 to 18 inches for large plants. Line wooden planters with rust-resistant metal or plastic liners. A floor lamp with a flexible "neck," or an expanding wall-bracket lamp, can be used as the light source. Or, you can let the potted plants remain in the planter for two or three weeks, then give them the same time under one of your fluorescent setups. When you garden the fluorescent way, you will soon have plenty of plants to create all kinds of pleasing displays around the house.

A tea cart filled with green and flowering plants can be kept in perfect condition under fluorescent lights. When you need a change of scenery in another room, simply wheel in your mobile garden.

Planter bins can be made in old chests, or tables. Plant greenery in a copper boiler or a wooden tub and you will be adding living beauty to your home.

I have even seen black cooking pots (the kind once used for outdoor cooking) transformed into handsome indoor planters for recreation rooms and country kitchens.

One of my friends has installed a 74-watt strip light under a picture windowsill and placed a long planter box under the light. This important indoor garden uses foliage plants for permanence, flowering plants in season for color and fragrance.

When you garden in planter boxes you save time. Grouping plants conserves moisture, and plants growing in plastic- or metal-lined bins do not dry out as rapidly as those growing in single pots. Once-a-month fertilizing is enough for most planter boxes.

Dish Gardens

Dish gardens that hold a collection of small plants make attractive display pieces for a buffet, a chest, or any table. There are thousands of plants from which to choose and the garden can be made in any dish or large pot saucer. Select plants that are compatible in cultural needs. For example, plant cacti and other succulents together; begonias, ferns, and miniature gloxinias; or use a miniature African violet as the focal point in a small garden, surrounded by creeping fig (*Ficus repens*) as a ground cover, a dwarf fern (*Polystichum tsus-simense*), and a young but treelike *Dracaena marginata*.

Treat dish gardens to a few hours of artificial light daily, or to invigorating, extended periods of under-light treatment, and these diminutive landscapes can be used to enhance dozens of places in your home.

When dishes lack drainage, cover the bottom with a layer of pebbles or pot chips and charcoal. The growing medium you use for potted specimens will suffice for a dish garden. Or, use the commercially prepared Black Magic Planter Mix, being sure to moisten it ahead of planting time, following directions on the package. Desert gardens need a gritty soil, as described in chapter 17.

Cacti and other succulents are particularly well suited to dish gardens. There is great diversity of form in these plants, and they require minimum attention in watering and fertilizing.

Many foliage plants are excellent subjects for dish gardening too. Some common kinds available at most local plant counters and florist shops include various peperomias, *Philodendron cordatum,* Chinese evergreen (aglaonema), small-leaved English ivies such as 'Merion Beauty,' and *Dracaena godseffiana*. Venturing to more unusual foliage plants for dish gardening—kinds you will probably want to order by mail from the specialists listed in chapter 22—consider cryptanthus, Kentia and other young palms, *Billbergia nutans,* maranta, calathea, homalomena, tillandsia, and young plants of unusual philodendrons, dieffenbachias, and dracaenas.

Terrariums and Other Under-Glass Gardens

The least demanding of all indoor gardens is a terrarium, a garden enclosed in glass. Here plants have ideal humidity and stay dust free. You can make a terrarium in a discarded aquarium with a glass cover, but many other glass containers can be changed into delightful terrariums. Brandy snifters, rose bowls, fish bowls, goblets, large jars and bottles, and stacked candy dishes—all make pretty under-glass gardens.

These gardens grow beautifully with a minimum of light. They're perfect for 20-watt fluorescents. And I once saw a most attractive bottle garden growing in a shadow box under a pencil-size fluorescent tube. Such tubes are available on order from lighting specialists.

Display your terrarium in low-light areas for a week or two, then give it an alternate, rejuvenating period under standard light setups.

To plant an aquarium or other glass container, pour a half to 1 inch of coarse gravel and perlite on the bottom. Add small pieces of charcoal. Cover with porous, moistened soil; a mixture of equal parts garden loam, peat moss, perlite, and vermiculite is excellent for dish gardening, except double the portions of loam and perlite for desert plants. If you fancy a woodland scene, mound some of the soil into hills; make depressions for valleys.

Select miniature, slow-growing plants, using only those that are compatible. Use a small piece of a mirror to give the illusion of water. Small pieces of driftwood can be used to support miniature vines. Small rocks and woodland moss or green sphagnum add a natural touch.

The Fine Art of Bottle Gardening

To plant a bottle garden, make it sparkling clean with a spraying of window cleaner. Wipe the spray off with a lintless cloth on a bent wire. Wait a day before making the garden because the fumes might be injurious to delicate plants.

Make a funnel of aluminum foil, or use a regular funnel. Insert in the bottle. Pour drainage material down the funnel, followed by some charcoal chips. Tap the bottle to settle the material. Add spoonfuls of moistened soil until the bottle is about one-fourth full. Firm the soil with a bent stick, wire or narrow tongs, then use any of these pieces of equipment to make planting holes. Remove plants from pots, wash all soil from the roots. Drop the plants into the bottle and firm the earth about them.

My favorite plants for closed bottle gardens are the selaginellas—including creeping as well as upright types. I like to combine them with a clump of *Sinningia pusilla,* the miniature gloxinia, but when the creeping selaginellas really get going, they will climb over the little gloxinias and smother them unless you exercise your tonsorial abilities, using a piece of razor blade inserted in the end of a long stick as your cutting tool.

Other plants with which I have been successful in bottle gardening include artillery plant (*Pilea microphylla*), variegated nephthytis, small ferns such as *Polystichum tsussimense,* strawberry-begonias (*Saxifraga sarmentosa* and its variegated variety *tricolor*), baby's-tears (*Helxine soleiroli*), miniature African violets, small-growing begonias ('Baby Perfectifolia,' 'Baby Rainbow,' 'Beatrice Haddrell,' 'Berry's Autumn,' 'Boweri,' 'Bow-Joe,' 'Calico,' 'Chantilly Lace,' 'China Doll,' 'Foliosa,' 'Griffithi,' *hydrocotylifolia,* 'It,' 'Kathy Diane,' 'Richard Robinson,' and 'Winter Jewel'), gloxineras (especially kinds like the Connecticut Hybrids), the silver orchid (*Erythroides nobilis argyrocentrus*), *Acorus gramineus variegatus*, allophyton, bertolonia, *Caladium humboldti*, calatheas, *Oxalis hedysaroides rubra*, *Haemaria discolor* var. *dawsoniana*, *Chamaeranthemum igneum* and *C. venosum*, fittonia, *Impatiens repens* and hybrids of *I. sultani* in dwarf-growing varieties such as 'Red Herold' and 'Orange Baby,' and pellionias.

If you have a minimum of time to spend with your glassed-in gardens, cover the tops with glass. This cuts down evaporation. Such under-glass gardens seldom need watering. Check them about once a month. If dry, water through a tube, drinking straw, or with a fine spray. Minus the glass they dry out faster and need more frequent watering.

If moisture beads form on the inside of covered gardens, remove the cover for a while. If possible, wipe the moisture from inside the glass before covering again.

Aquatic Gardens and Aquariums

If you'd like an indoor garden but do not want to be bothered with soil and potting, decorate with beautiful greenery growing in water. Most of the plants that grow well in water gardens are low-light types, but all of the water gardens grow lushly when they receive the benefit of at least four hours of artificial light each day, or when given an occasional sojourn under the lights.

Decorative bottles, vases, shells, brandy snifters, or glass bricks with openings in them provide suitable and interesting containers. English ivy, philodendron, dracaena, pickaback (tolmiea), Chinese evergreen (aglaonema), nephthytis, pothos, and coleus are a few of the plants that thrive in water. Another favorite of mine is the plectranthus, a relative of the coleus, with trailing habit that's well suited to water culture.

Knock the plant from its pot, crumble the soil away, then rinse the roots in running lukewarm water. Nonrusting needle holders will keep large plants upright in containers. Stones and small shells will hold others in place. Small pieces of charcoal will keep the water fresh-smelling. Colored glass or plastic bubbles, or bright beads, add decorator touches to clear glass containers. These really bring sparkling translucent color under agricultural lamps such as Gro-Lux.

If you raise tropical fish and the aquatic greenery that makes up part of the underwater scene, add fluorescent or incandescent light above the tank and the plants will take on new life and vigor. Many of the fish take on fantastic coloring under the agricultural lamps.

Recommended lighting for a 10-gallon tank is one or two 25-watt incandescent showcase lights or a 14-watt fluorescent. Many hobbyists feel they get the best results from warm white fluorescents. If the aquarium is in a cool, dark place, burn the lights about eight hours daily. If it is in a sunny area or if algae forms too rapidly, cut down on the size of the lights or the number of light hours.

Waterscaping a fluorescent-lighted aquarium can be an exciting venture. Right from the beginning there is fascination as you select from the host of suitable plants, most of which have strange-sounding names. For example, there will be vallisneria (eel grass), sagittaria (arrowhead), cryptocoryne, sword plant, cabomba (fanwort), myriophyllum (milfoil), anacharis (elodea), duckweed, nitella, water sprite, hairgrass, banana plant, hornwort, and bacopa. I have enjoyed the lavender-blue flowers of water hyacinth in a fluorescent-lighted aquarium, even though this plant is the curse of southern waterways.

The most recent of all developments in the world of phytoillumination and aquatics is a small-growing, hybrid water lily called 'Margaret Mary,' introduced by Three Springs Fisheries of Lilypons, Maryland. The flowers are light blue with a yellow center, and the plant can be cultivated year-round in an aquarium that receives about fourteen hours of illumination daily from fluorescent lamps.

Gardens That Spark Conversation

If you enjoy novelty plants, try some with built-in buds or unique growth habits for your under-light garden. There are some bulbs that flower without soil, but they do better, of course, when potted in a soil mixture such as equal parts garden loam, peat moss, and vermiculite. For example, the colchicums, bulbous plants with purple or yellow cupped flowers, which are often advertised as "wonder plants" because in autumn the bulbs, in or out of soil, will flower at the appointed time. This one is poisonous, so keep it out of reach of children and pets.

Amorphophallus rivieri, a giant aroid known by such mysterious names as "Voodoo Lily," sends out a huge dark-reddish-brown "flower" (the *spathe*) with a slender, dark-red *spadix* or column rising from the center. This plant is unique and will cause much comment, but it has a most disagreeable odor. I have seen these giants grow 4 to 6 feet tall. Therefore you will have to devise some means of raising the fluorescent fixture, or lowering the amorphophallus. Four or five hours of artificial light per day will keep the scape sturdy and straight. Plant outdoors in the summer in rich, well-drained soil. Select a site that is protected from midday sun and strong winds. The palmlike foliage will add a touch of the tropics to any setting. Dig and bring inside before frost in autumn.

Lily-of-the-valley pips that you order by mail in autumn arrive already precooled and ready to grow. They're usually potted in light soil or sphagnum moss. Place them under any of your light setups and you will soon have the fragrance of spring in your winter garden.

The air plant (bryophyllum, or by some authorities,

kalanchoe) survives for a while on air alone; for example, when pinned to a curtain. However, it grows into an interesting plant when potted in soil. Small plantlets form on edges of the leaves, drop to the soil, and grow. If you have a tray of moist pebbles or vermiculite on which you place the containers of your fluorescent-lighted garden, these airborne plantlets may form a small forest in an amazingly short time.

The resurrection plant (*Selaginella lepidophylla*) is a dry, gray-green ball. When placed in a saucer of water or a pot of moistened soil it expands into a flat green rosette. It can be alternately dried off and revived by letting it become dry, then providing moisture. Children of all ages are fascinated by this unusual plant.

10

Gift Plants in Lighted Gardens

Some gift plants are lasting treasures, others are to be enjoyed while they flower, and then discarded. These brilliantly flowered plants have been reared in a greenhouse under ideal conditions of light, temperature, and humidity. If you have well-lighted windows in your home, you can keep them flowering. If you provide them with twelve to sixteen hours of fluorescent light daily, you will have the pleasure of watching all the buds grow and burst into full bloom. With a little know-how you can enjoy yearly performances from many gift plants.

To Keep or Not to Keep

Calceolaria, cineraria, and primroses are gift plants that are best treated as expendables—discard when they finish flowering. All three need ample watering, cool temperatures, and a moist atmosphere. It's easier in most homes to keep them crisp and colorful under lights.

Azaleas can be kept for years. Hardy types (the florist should know which kind you received) can be grown year-round in gardens south of Washington, D.C., provided your other climatic conditions besides cold are hospitable. Plant outdoors in humusy soil that is richly laced with acid peat moss and well-rotted leaf mold. If you live in the north, shift azaleas to a larger pot, plunge outdoors in summer, bring into a cool, 50-degree room in the fall, and keep the soil lightly moistened (never really dry) until December or January. Then move to a light setup employing at least a pair of 40-watt fluorescents burned twelve to sixteen hours daily. Keep well watered and feed monthly with an iron chelate such as Sequestrene or a specially prepared fertilizer for acid-loving plants.

Camellia, with its round, richly hued flowers, is seldom grown in northern gardens. A Chicago, Illinois, grower who recognized that these plants offered a challenge to under-light gardeners, has successfully flowered several varieties under lights. Another grower says he has flowered camellias under a bank of four 40-watt strip lights (two agricultural lamps, two natural tubes) burned sixteen hours a day. Plants are fogged every day to increase humidity and they are growing in an acid soil in a cool basement.

Easter lilies, kept under fluorescent tubes, stay firm and straight. When summer arrives plant them outdoors. They are hardy and with average garden culture they will give you a yearly show of blooms in late spring. If you want to force some Easter lilies under lights, do it in one of your cooler growing areas. They'll grow and bloom under six-teen to eighteen hours of light from a pair of 40-watt tubes with temperatures up to 70 degrees, but leaves may yellow and the stems become spindly in too much heat. I've had fair success growing these bulbs at 68 degrees, but they are really superb at a cool 55 degrees.

It takes three to four months for the bulbs to bloom. Pot at soil level in 6-inch pots. Water, and store for three or four weeks in a dark, 55- to 60-degree area. When growth shows, bring to the light, keep well watered, and fertilize weekly. You will be thrilled, I am sure, when your first lily blooms under lights and the fragrance permeates the house. A new super-dwarf Easter lily called 'Snow White' has recently been introduced in this country. This variety promises to be ideal for under-light gardens since total height, even in full flower, is only 10 inches. Grow it from seeds sown in your lighted garden at any season.

Fuchsias need night temperatures below 65 degrees to set flower buds. If possible, summer them in a shaded location outdoors. These plants usually rest in early fall and part of the winter. Give them a cool growing area while they are in this semidormancy. When new growth shows, place them under a pair of 40-watt fluorescents and fertilize biweekly. The honeysuckle fuchsia, sometimes called 'Gartenmeister Bohnstedt,' is much easier to handle indoors than most recent hybrids. It will grow well among plants requiring daytime temperatures of 65 to 70 degrees, and makes a constant display of bright red flowers.

Gardenias, pearly white and richly perfumed, can be vexing indeed, for they drop buds at the slightest provocation. Don't be dismayed if your gift plant sheds buds. Concentrate on keeping the plant in glowing health, learn its requirements, and you will be able to bring it into flower in successive years.

How to Grow Gardenias

Whenever possible, summer gardenias on a porch or in the sheltered garden. Best temperatures for indoor growth are 70 to 75 degrees during the day, with a drop to a range of 62 to 65 at night. Keep soil moist, humidity high. When repotting use soil with an acid reaction; equal parts loam, sand, and peat moss should do the trick, unless you live in an area of alkaline soil. Feed biweekly from January to September, alternating between a balanced houseplant fertilizer and a solution of 1 ounce ammonium sulfate mixed in 2 gallons of water. Plants in need of fertilizer or those growing in daytime temperatures under 60 degrees may show chlorosis, that is, yellowing leaves.

Gardenia bud drop may be caused from a number of environmental conditions: overwatering, lack of humidity, or night temperatures above 70 or below 60 degrees.

Young holly plants are popular Christmas gifts that grow lustily under 40-watt fluorescents. Grown with other foliage plants and given but four to six hours of artificial illumination daily, they stay pretty but grow slowly. Growth proceeds naturally and shinier leaves result when given twelve to sixteen hours of light per day. Holly needs acid soil and plants are touchy about transplanting. Transplant in early spring to well-drained pots. When new growth starts, alternate fertilizing between an all-purpose fertilizer and a special type for acid-loving plants.

Citrus—orange, lemon, lime, and tangerine—grow luxuriantly under fluorescents. Twelve to sixteen hours of light daily, water enough to keep the soil always moist, and daytime temperatures around 72 to 75 degrees will aid them in producing the fragrant flowers. If you want fruit on indoor plants, remove the pollen from one flower and place it on the stigma of another. Plants summering outdoors will be pollinated by insects. Twice-a-month feedings with all-purpose fertilizer stimulate growth. If leaves turn yellow, water the plant with an iron chelate solution such as Sequestrene.

Cyclamen, with its long-lasting shooting-star flowers and handsome gray-green patterned leaves, is a difficult plant to force into rebloom. Grow it in a cool room with at least sixteen hours of light per day. Withhold water after flowering and rest nearly dry during the summer in basement or shaded garden area. Repot in the fall into equal parts garden loam, sand, and peat moss. Keep the corm at its former level. The soil needs to be slightly moistened until growth shows; then place the plant under lights and hope for the best. A much surer way to have cyclamen flowers is to plant seeds in the fall. Seedlings will bloom under lights in about eighteen months.

Frankly, I don't like to spend the time necessary to make

Christmas begonias such as 'Melior,' 'Gloire de Lorraine,' 'Lady Mac,' and other similar types rebloom. It's easier to take cuttings from the plants, root them, and grow under ten to twelve hours of light daily. Some of the cuttings will flower when they are but 3 inches high. To develop really sturdy plants for the holidays, start short, stocky cuttings from basal growth in the spring. Grow under the lights on sixteen-hour days until about September. Then shorten day length to ten or twelve hours for Christmas bloom.

Hydrangeas are beautiful but much too shrubby for average under-light gardens. Keep soil abundantly moist; the large leaves droop at even a hint of dryness. When blooms fade, cut back the stems halfway. If winter temperatures in your climate stay generally above 20 degrees, transplant your hydrangea outdoors when danger of frost passes in the spring. Otherwise, discard. I would never attempt to rebloom the florists' hydrangea indoors, and, unfortunately, my climate is too cold in the winter to successfully grow this type outdoors.

Poinsettias, too, are difficult to bring into flower in lighted gardens. Keep soil evenly moist, protect from chilling or drying drafts, and provide daytime temperatures from 65 to 72 degrees. When the colorful bracts (commonly called "petals") fall, set the plant where temperatures will not go below 55 degrees. Keep the soil lightly moistened. Repot into fresh soil in the spring. When weather warms, plunge the pot in the outdoor garden.

Take poinsettia cuttings of new growth from June until August. Root in moist sand or vermiculite. When roots have formed, pot in equal parts garden loam, peat moss, and sand. Bring the young plants into the house before frost. Place them under lights but you may have to devise a special program for these short-day plants. They require at least twelve hours of *complete* darkness out of every twenty-four; even a small ray of light during this critical period will prevent flowering at the holiday season. Move them to a completely dark room or cover them from 5 in the afternoon to 7 the next morning. A black sateen cloth makes good shading. Shade from October 10 to 20 and you may be fortunate enough to have your own poinsettias flowering for Christmas.

11

African Violets—Artificial Light Pioneers

African violets were among the first plants to be grown successfully under lights. These lushly foliaged, heavily flowered light-grown plants created quite a problem at an early show. They were so far superior to the window-grown plants that it didn't seem fair to exhibit them in the same classes. After this initial exhibit African violets grown under artificial light had to be entered in special classes where window-grown plants would not be competing against them. This has changed today, since most exhibitors grow at least some of their African violets under fluorescents.

African violets are not real violets. The botanical name is *Saintpaulia* and they belong to the *Gesneriaceae*. Popular gesneriad relatives include gloxinias, episcias, and achimenes.

Although thousands of growers produce splendid Saintpaulias in well-lighted east or north windows, these tractable plants simply outdo themselves when grown under fluorescent lights. Here foliage grows thick and glossy, petioles (leaf stems) shorten, and flowers are produced abundantly. With a wise growing and propagating program these adaptable plants respond with flowers year-round.

If African violets are a new love with you, if you are not satisfied with the performance of your window-grown violets, or your collection has exceeded available window space, try growing them under fluorescent lights.

Species and Hybrids

Baron Walter von Saint Paul-Illaire, of Berlin, discovered *Saintpaulia ionantha* and other species in 1892. So fascinated was he with these handsome little purple- and blue-flowered plants which he found growing in the hills of eastern tropical Africa, that he sent seeds of the plants to his father, Hofsmarschal Baron von Saint Paul of Fischbach in Silesia, a man who was also keenly interested in horticulture. He grew plants from the seed and presented them to the Royal Botanical Gardens. Here the director, Herman Wendland, named the plant in honor of the son and father Saint Paul, calling it *Saintpaulia ionantha*, "with violetlike flowers." Plants were exhibited at the 1893 International Horticultural Exhibit in Ghent. This unpretentious plant with its violetlike flowers and an exotic orchid were named the "two most botanically interesting plants in the exhibition."

Mr. Ernst Benary, commercial plantsman in Erfurt, Germany, realized the popular appeal of the saintpaulia and started propagating it from seed. Soon he developed wine, white, and various blue and purple varieties.

Plant explorers continued discovering new species, and hybridizers developed still more varieties. Today's specialists list about twenty species and thousands of hybrids.

If your aim is to collect interesting African violets or to hybridize smaller, larger, different-colored or more floriferous violets, why not explore the wide possibilities offered by the species, ancestors of our favorite hybrids?

I have grown twelve of the species under lights. It is a special pleasure to compare them with hybrid forms, and to sort out traits that the hybrids have inherited from species.

S. amaniensis, endemic to the valleys of the Usambara Mountains, sends up small violet-blue flowers above pointed green leaves. Leaf undersides are near white and the upper surface is covered with a mixture of long and short hairs. It is nearly impossible to make this naturally multiple-crowned violet into a single-crowned specimen. It is at its best when grown in a moist, cool area and grows superbly with less light than we give some of the hybrids. Here's one you can safely place near the end zones of the tubes and it's a natural for growing in a cool basement setup.

Professional reports on *S. confusa* list the blossoms as being an inch across. The dark violet clusters on my plants have flowers measuring about three-fourths inch wide. The bright lettuce-green leaves have serrated or saw-toothed margins. *S. confusa* is a bounteous bloomer growing into a large, many-crowned plant. Like many other thin-leaved plants, it prospers best when grown with less light. Try growing it on the outer edges of your light setups or under smaller 20-watt units.

Rather hairy purplish leaves and pale-lavender flowers distinguish the true *S. diplotricha* from *S. confusa.* When this species gets too much light its upper leaf sides turn olive drab.

Single-crowned *S. grandifolia* displays a shower of dark-purple blooms over its satiny green leaves. This handsome species is easily handled under average care, growing flat and symmetrical when placed about 10 to 12 inches from 40-watt lights.

Versatile *S. grotei* can be grown as a climber or a trailer. Its rounded leaves are produced on long reddish-brown stems and its flowers are light blue at the petal tips, shading to darker centers. Seedpods on this one often grow to an inch and a half in length. This species has many possibilities for the plant breeder. In my collection I have single and double pink hybrids which had *S. grotei* as one parent.

Neither of these hybrids has the reddish stems nor the climbing or trailing habit of the species parent.

Saintpaulia ionantha was one of the first forms discovered by Baron von Saint Paul-Illaire. A large, spreading plant, it often shows as many as eight blue-violet flowers in clusters held high over thick, dark-green, quilted leaves. Temperatures in Tanga, its homeland, average 80 degrees, and it seems to have passed down heat tolerance to the progeny.

S. intermedia is aptly named, for its growth habits are midway between the rosette types and the trailers. Its small, light-blue flowers are borne on short stems over spooned or cupped, olive-green leaves.

Round, hairy, cupped-down leaves, creeping stems, and medium violet-blue flowers characterize *S. magungensis*. If your breeding aims include plants with leaves which curve over the pot edge, you will want to add this one to your stock.

Numerous crowns of thin, green, heart-shaped leaves and small lavender flowers borne in abundance distinguish *S. orbicularis*. Hailing from the West Usambara Mountains where daytime temperatures may reach 90 degrees, then drop to below 50 at night, this obliging species has a built-in tolerance for a wide range of growing conditions.

If you like small plants you will enjoy miniature *S. shumensis*. The petite olive-green leaves have light red undersides. Near-white flowers have a dainty blotch of purple on the upper petals. Easy does it when watering this one, for it is native to a dry area in the mountains.

S. tongewensis has thick, hairy, tapering leaves which may be red or light green underneath. Its purple flowers are slightly over an inch wide. A naturally flat grower, it can stand the maximum amount of artificial light you accord your violets.

S. velutina is generous with its pale-blue white-tipped flowers. Its velvety heart-shaped leaves have pretty red reverses.

There are other interesting ones, too, which you may find for your collection. *S. goetzeana* produces rosettes of dark leaves and lavender flowers. I have had this one several times, but it has never stayed long enough for me to discover the culture needed. Successful growers say it should be grown cooler than other species and with decreased light. And it appears to require higher humidity than can be supplied in most homes.

S. difficilis has slightly spooned willow-green leaves and it bears a heavy crop of medium-blue flowers. *S. inconspicua* is a trailer with small white flowers. Purple-flowered *S. nitida* has glossy oval leaves and brown petioles. *S. pendula* has round, firm, gray-green leaves and blue flowers. Miniature *S. pusilla* is only 5 inches wide. The small, blunt leaves have red-purple undersides and the small bicolored flowers are blue and white—a treasure for the hybridizer who wants to produce more miniatures. *S. teitensis* is reported to have leaves growing from a "long, unbranched stalk."

Thousands of saintpaulia cultivars or varieties have been introduced. It would be useless to list them, for by the time this book is published today's most popular varieties would have been superseded by still newer beauties. Plain, dark-green-leaved varieties are sometimes called "boy" types. Leaves with a pale greenish-white spot at the base are referred to as "girl" types. These terms do not refer to the sex of the plant, because African violets have bisexual flowers. Leaves may be plain, waved, or ruffled with serrate or crenate (scalloped) edges in all shades of green, from chartreuse to near black, with or without red reverses. There are even some variegated varieties with white and green or white, green, and pink leaves. Flowers are single or double with plain or frilled petals in white, and many hues of pink, purple, and blue. Some varieties produce pink and purple flowers on the same plant and there are kinds that bear flowers half purple and half pink. The bicolors shade from one color to another. To date there are no yellow saintpaulias, but hybridizers have made great strides in other fields of breeding these plants. The violet-shaped flower, for example, has been displaced in many modern varieties by a perfect star shape. Size is increasing, floriferous qualities are improving, and there are radiant or "hot" pinks that fairly sparkle with vibrant coloring.

If you are just starting a saintpaulia collection, visit a greenhouse and choose varieties you find most appealing. Or send for specialists' catalogs and order the types which you believe will be most pleasing. Many African violet growers issue beautifully illustrated catalogs.

Phytoillumination and African Violets

African violets thrive under any of the white, natural, or daylight fluorescents as well as the lavender-tinted agricultural lamps such as Gro-Lux.

While preparing this manuscript I interviewed many gardeners who grow violets under lights and I observed thousands of the plants in fluorescent-lighted gardens from New York to California, and Minneapolis to Miami. With such a great selection of fluorescents from which to choose, it is no wonder the new grower may hesitate in choosing lights which will give him the most satisfaction. A few of the growers interviewed frankly prefer the glamorous effect given plants by the lavender agricultural lamps. These persons delight in the dark, glowing green of the foliage, and the vivid, near-red appearance of pink and rose flowers. Many commercial growers object to the lights on these same grounds, feeling that when plants are removed from the lights to natural light, the customer is dissatisfied with the color change.

No doubt personal preference will influence your choice of lights. No matter the choice, your light-grown African violets will give you tremendous pleasure.

One of my favorite combinations for growing African violets is a pair of 40-watt tubes, one warm white, the other an agricultural lamp. The plants grow rapidly and bloom profusely. The single lavender-hued lamp adds just the right touch of glamor to make plants appear at their best.

Basic Light Setup for African Violets

Suspend a pair of 40-watt fluorescent tubes and a reflector 18 inches above a table or other growing area. This will light a growing space 2 × 4 feet, giving you room for approximately eighteen violets in 4-inch pots, or dozens of seedlings, cuttings, and small plants in 1- to 3-inch pots.

Space mature plants 10 to 15 inches from the 40-watt tubes; 7 to 9 inches from 20-watters. Leave the lights on twelve to sixteen hours daily. Violets receiving more light than this may become malformed.

You will soon discover your plants' requirements. As a general rule, African violets with pink or white flowers, girl foliage, or light-colored leaves need less light than the darker flowered and foliaged kinds. Set the plants that need most light in the center and directly under the tubes; use the end zones and side areas for plants with lesser light requirements.

Large, thick-leaved 'Amazon' and 'Supreme' varieties need all the light they can get to make them flower well. Where to place the variegated types poses a problem. The plants need the chlorophyll to grow and as the plant increases in size and vigor the green coloring often takes over, leaving little if any of the attractive white or pink variegation. At least one well-known grower has reported success growing these temperamental plants under the new agricultural lamps.

African violets with long willowy leaves and sparse bloom need more light. If you leave the lights on for the recommended length of time, boost these plants closer to the tubes. Plants showing bleached foliage, shortened petioles, and flower stalks may be receiving too much light. Move them away from the light tubes, or decrease the number of light hours.

Under-Light Culture of African Violets

There are many schools of thought on the correct soil for African violets. A standard one which is easy to make is composed of equal parts garden loam, sand (or perlite), leaf mold (or vermiculite), and peat moss. However, almost any soil that is porous and humusy will do for violets. Some growers produce glorious plants in nothing but vermiculite or perlite. These saintpaulias need a weekly fertilizing program since inorganic substances merely support the plants in the pots, but provide no nutrition.

If you do not want to mix soil, or if the ingredients are not readily available, try one of the prepared mixtures manufactured for African violets. You will find packaged mediums at local garden centers, or you can buy them by mail from African violet specialists listed in chapter 22.

If you mix your own soil, sterilize it to prevent nematode infestation. Instructions are included in chapter 6.

While some of the species saintpaulias grow naturally in temperatures down in the 40s and up into the 90s, potted violets will thrive with daytime temperatures of 70 to 75 degrees, and a drop of about 10 degrees at night.

Growers who prefer running lights at night now have scientific evidence which bears out the theory that African violets grow and bloom better when temperature changes are reversed, that is, the low temperature used in the daytime, the higher temperature at night.

While at the Earhart Laboratory for Plant Research, Pasadena, California, Dr. Frits W. Went, Director, conducted an experiment for the African Violet Society of America, and reported it in the *African Violet Magazine*. His findings show that a high day temperature and a low night temperature were poor growing and flowering conditions for saintpaulia. In the experiment the best plants were obtained by growing them at 60 to 68 degrees during the day and 70 to 75 degrees at night.

Since most hobbyists like to have the fun of experimenting with plants, why not try this reverse temperature idea, starting with basement-grown plants where it is easier to reverse day and night darkness, and, in some cases, cool temperatures?

Humidity of 50 per cent is ideal but impossible in some homes. Even 40 per cent is sufficient for satisfactory African violet culture. Ideas for increasing moisture content of the air surrounding your plants may be found in chapter 5.

Keep the leaves clean by brushing them with a soft camel's-hair brush (never a hairbrush) or by taking them to the sink, rinsing off the dust with a spray of tepid water, and returning them to the lights. Never put wet-leaved violets in the sun, for rays shining on water drops burn holes in the leaves. Fluorescent rays will not cause this burning.

Good air circulation is an inducement to flowering. Poor air circulation, such as exists in basements, may cause mildew on plants and soil. Most growers having basement plant rooms keep the air moving with circulating fans. Exhaust fans are sometimes needed also.

How and when to water your plants can be a touchy problem. Even experienced growers sometimes over- or under-water. Be guided by these simple rules: Push your finger into the soil. If the medium feels damp or moist at the half-inch mark, the plant doesn't need watering. If it feels dry, apply water. Always use water of room temperature and apply from either the top or bottom. Don't water again until the soil is approaching dryness.

After you've grown African violets awhile you will decide

on a watering and fertilizing program which fits in with your area and the time you can spend with your plants.

While it is possible to have flowering saintpaulias the year around, many gardeners like to give the plants a rest in the summer and bring them into heavy bloom for the fall and winter months. This is especially true in southernmost areas where summer months are hot.

For year-round flowers, fertilize all plants, both small and large, at biweekly intervals, using one-fourth to one-half strength fertilizer on the young plants. If you want to rest the plants in summer, keep them watered, omit the fertilizer, and start your feeding program again in September.

How to Propagate Favorite African Violets

African violets are propagated through leaves, plant division, or the fine, dustlike seed. Light-grown plants will flower in four to six months from cuttings; six to nine months from seed (see chapter 7). When propagating a variegated-leaved variety, use leaves having some green coloring in them. Pure white leaves soon wither and die. If you are hybridizing African violets with variegated types in mind, use a variegated plant as the seed parent.

Bugs and Other African Violet Bothers

If good cultural rules are followed, annoyances are few with light-grown African violets, but woe to the grower who fails to give plants the proper soil, water, fertilizer, and light they need. Under poor growing conditions, African violets are subject to attack from aphids, cyclamen mites, broad mites, plant and soil mealybugs, nematodes, red spider mites, springtails, and thrips (see chapter 8). Don't let this list scare you. Think of the lengthy list of ailments we humans are prone to, many of which can be avoided or overcome when we receive proper food and rest.

African violets are also subject to crown rot, petiole rot, and leaf ring spot. These grievances can happen to violets growing in any kind of light.

Plants having crown rot show limp leaves hanging over the pot edge, appearing in need of a good drink of water. But this is just what they don't need. Chances are they've had more water than they can use. Best way to restore such plants to health is to remove them from the pot, cut away limp outer leaves and repot in fresh soil. If this method has been unsuccessful for you, simply wash the soil from the roots, cut away limp leaves, and reroot the plant in water, vermiculite, or perlite. When well rooted, replant in fresh soil.

Dark, mushy, outer leaf stalks or petioles with rusty marks have petiole rot from the fertilizer salts which have collected on the pot rim. Avoid this by covering pot rims with foil or one of the specially designed rubber pot rims. If you prefer seeing the natural pot look, remove the whitish deposit of fertilizer salts. A metal Chore Boy or steel wool and soap pad will do the trick. Rid the soil of excess fertilizer by giving the plant several copious waterings during the same day. Then be sparing on the fertilizer until the plant seems to have recovered.

Leaf ring spot results when there is a great difference between the temperature of the air and the water. Always apply water of room temperature and avoid spilling it on the leaves.

Burning and bunching occurs when plants are receiving too much light. Although fluorescents are "cool" light they do give off enough heat to burn leaves which come in direct contact with them. When centers of plants grow bunched and knotty, it does not always mean the plant has cyclamen mites. If you have checked such a plant with a hand lens and cannot find any mites, the plant may be receiving more light than it can use. Give such plants less light by moving them farther from the light source. Be sure they are never receiving more than sixteen hours of light in any twenty-four-hour period. If you do not use an automatic timer, and lights are left on continuously for several days and nights, malformed growth will result.

Light Shock Treatment

The newest innovation in African violet culture is something called an "eighty-four-hour shock treatment." This is recommended by one successful grower of my acquaintance for a plant in good health that for no apparent reason grows slowly or fails to bloom. Maintain the usual balance of light and dark periods before and after the treatment, and resort to it only if you are certain that the plant is in perfect health.

12

Everyone Can Grow Gloxinias the Fluorescent Way

A flowering gloxinia with velvety bells of glowing color or spotless white brings new excitement to lighted gardens. Gloxinias are grown as summertime florist crops or spring and summer window-garden plants, but you can have them in flower all year in a fluorescent-lighted garden.

Technically speaking, the florists' gloxinia is not a gloxinia. It is a gesneriad belonging to the genus *Sinningia*. It was named gloxinia in 1785 in honor of P. B. Gloxin of Strassburg, Germany. Botanists didn't discover until 1825 that another gesneriad had been christened *Gloxinia* early in the 1700s. By the time this mistake had come to light, the name was so firmly entrenched in the minds of the many gardeners who had grown these lovely plants that they didn't bother to change the name.

Gloxinia perennis, the true gloxinia, is a tall plant with bell-shaped lavender-blue flowers. It grows from a scaly rhizome, rather than a tuber, and height makes it less suited to under-light gardening than the sinningias.

Start with Firm Gloxinia Tubers

Gloxinias (meaning species and hybrids of sinningia) grow from tubers that resemble small potatoes. At time of purchase, these vary in size from 1 to 3 inches across, but size at this stage really has very little to do with the eventual flower crop. It is tuber firmness that counts. *Sinningia pusilla,* the miniature gloxinia, may have tubers the size of a pea or as large as a nickel.

Pot large tubers in 5- or 6-inch pots. I use shallow bulb pans or azalea pots. Some of my gloxinias grow in pure unmilled sphagnum moss combined with biweekly feedings; others grow in a mixture of equal parts garden loam, peat moss, sand (or perlite), and leaf mold (or vermiculite).

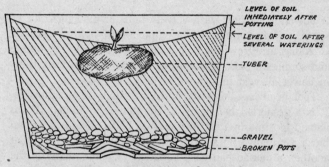

Figure 4. How to pot a gloxinia tuber.

Either way gives the results I expect. Fill the pot to within about 2 inches of the top with the growing medium. Center the tuber, indented side up, then cover until the medium is about one-half inch from the top. Water well, then set in a warm spot (60 degrees minimum). Ideally, this will be under a fluorescent setup of two 20-watt, two 40-watt, or two 74-watt tubes, where the cultivation of other plants helps maintain a moist atmosphere. Gentle bottom heat of 70 to 80 degrees hastens rooting. Keep the soil slightly moist until the leaves begin showing. If you have started the tuber in a shaded place, now is the time to move it to the lights.

Lighted FloraCart in author's living room provides 24 square feet of growing space for ferns, coleus, amaryllis, African violets, gloxinias, episcias, begonias, geraniums, bromeliads, and *Scilla violacea*. (NICHOLSON)

Lighted FloraCarts in St. Paul basement of University of Minnesota geneticist Dr. Sheldon C. Reed provide 168 square feet of growing space— equivalent to a 10 x 16 home greenhouse. (MEL JACOBSEN)

Closeup view of Dr. Reed's fluorescent-grown African violets. (JACOBSEN)

Antonelli hybrid gloxinias, typical of those that can be grown under fluorescent-light culture. (GEIGER, courtesy PARK'S FLORAL MAGAZINE)

African violet 'Miss Atlantic City' from Fischer Greenhouses, Linwood, New Jersey, takes on unusual radiance when grown with agricultural lamps such as Gro-Lux. (FISCHER GREENHOUSES)

Collection of achimenes flowers, grown under fluorescent lights, and arranged at the George W. Park Seed Company, Greenwood, South Carolina. (PARK)

Picotee hybrid tuberous begonia from Antonelli Brothers, typical of those that can be brought into out-of-season bloom in lighted gardens.

Double rose form tuberous begonia hybrid, also from Antonelli, shows another flower type that can be cultivated under lights.

Spring comes early in a fluorescent-lighted garden; cyclamen, azaleas, daffodils, and hyacinths put on a colorful and fragrant display. (SELECT STUDIOS)

Daffodils, azalea, hyacinths, Dutch irises, and tulips forced into early bloom in fluorescent-lighted garden. (SELECT STUDIOS)

Cymbidium orchid Miretta 'Dos Pueblos' needs nighttime temperature around 50–55 degrees, fresh, moist air, and an evenly moist growing medium of shredded firbark. (DOS PUEBLOS ORCHID COMPANY)

Magic carpet of coleus 'Brilliant' cultivated from seeds under fluorescent lights. (GEO. W. PARK SEED CO.)

Calla-lily begonia 'Calla Queen' is a semperflorens type that may be grown from seeds in a fluorescent-lighted garden. (GEO. W. PARK SEED CO.)

Gloxinias grow thriftily under many kinds of light setups. If you are a beginner, place them about 8 inches from the center of a pair of 40-watt fluorescents and burn the lights sixteen hours a day. As with African violets and other gesneriads, I have successfully grown these tropical beauties under many kinds, sizes, and combinations of lights: one daylight and one natural; one daylight and one plant-growth lamp such as Gro-Lux; two growth lamps; or one cool white and one daylight. Personally I dislike growing gloxinias under setups involving incandescent light. I find it difficult to keep humidity at a 50 per cent level with these lights, but other growers have reported success with setups that use both types of light.

Keep gloxinia soil nicely moist. It should feel springy, but never soggy, to the touch. Fertilize biweekly as soon as growth becomes active, using any houseplant food diluted in water and applied according to container directions. Your gloxinia should flower in three or four months. Keep watering it as long as new growth continues around the base. When growth stops, decrease the water supply until the soil is nearly dry.

Store the tuber in the pot in a dark closet or other area where the temperature is about 50 to 60 degrees. Check resting tubers weekly and sprinkle the topsoil with water to keep it from becoming bone dry. This treatment assures firm tubers from one season to another. When new growth shows, repot in fresh soil and begin a new growing cycle.

Gloxinia Problems Solved

A well-grown gloxinia is a flat, symmetrical plant. (There are two exceptions among the species.) If your gloxinia grows tall and spindly, or trails over the edge of the pot, it is not receiving enough light. You can stake the plant and move it closer to the lights, or cut off the top, thus forcing the tuber to send out new growth. You can root the cut parts and have still more gloxinias.

Gloxinia leaf curl is associated with dry air, dim light, low temperature, or, in some cases, heredity. Flecks or spots of white on the leaves often result when cold water is sprinkled on them, or used to moisten the growing medium.

If buds brown and wither, check all points of good gloxinia culture. Be sure that water is applied to the soil surface, not directly on the crown of buds. Provide at least 40 to 50 per cent relative humidity around the plants. Adequate air circulation is vital, but avoid drafts of cold or very hot air. Broad mites, thrips, mealybugs, and cyclamen mites may also cause buds to blast. I deal with thrips and mealybugs by spraying with an aerosol of African violet pesticide. Mites, fortunately, have never attacked my gloxinias, but other growers recommend the use of sodium selenate in the soil. This systemic is a deadly poison that must be used cautiously.

Occasionally a gloxinia tuber develops rot, owing to excess moisture in the soil, combined with excessively high or low temperatures. And in isolated cases, root nematodes may destroy a gloxinia. Either of these problems is best dealt with by destroying the ailing plant, soil, tuber, and all. Sterilize the pots before using again.

How to Increase Gloxinias

It's fun to propagate gloxinias. You can grow more of them from leaves, tip cuttings, tuber divisions, or seeds. Leaves, cuttings, and divisions root speedily in moist vermiculite or milled sphagnum moss. Cuttings flower in eight to twelve months. Tuber divisions flower as quickly as complete tubers. Seedlings open first blooms in four to six months.

The smallest leaves root most rapidly, produce smaller tubers, and generally flower ahead of older, larger leaves.

Insert the leaf stem into a small pot of rooting medium, or place several leaves in a propagating box, large pot, or pan. Cover the planting with glass or polyethylene and place under the lights (near the end zones will be fine if you are crowded for space), and you have the makings of new gloxinia tubers. When moisture beads form inside the cover, remove, wipe dry, then replace. Some leaves will die down after the tuber has formed. Others send out a number of new plants while the original leaf is still green. Treat small dormant tubers as you would large ones; water lightly until you see new growth. Then plant in a 4-inch pot of soil.

Gloxinias of all kinds—the species, slipper-flowered sinningias, to the fanciest large, frilled singles and doubles—grow readily from seeds. These may be started at any season under fluorescent lights. Sow on the surface of moist, milled sphagnum moss or vermiculite. Moisten by adding water from a teaspoon. Cover with glass or polyethylene to keep the seeds evenly moist at all times. This is vital. Place about 5 inches beneath fluorescent tubes burned fourteen to sixteen hours daily, and in a temperature range of 65 to 75 degrees. After germination, remove the covering. When the first true leaves develop, transplant 1×1 inch in a community pot or flat, or to individual $2\frac{1}{4}$-inch pots. At this stage you can use unmilled sphagnum moss as the growing medium, combined with weekly feedings of Hyponex mixed at the rate of 1 teaspoon per gallon of water; or you can plant seedlings in your usual gloxinia potting soil. As soon as seedlings begin to crowd, transplant to individual 4- or 5-inch pots.

Species and Slipper Gloxinias

Start your gloxinia collection with the species and slippers. They have stamina, grow easily, and produce a bumper flower crop. Include the miniature *Sinningia pusilla*, the handsome-leaved *S. regina,* and the floriferous *S. eumorpha.* The more difficult *S. tubiflora,* with pebbled green leaves and fragrant flowers, needs high light intensity to bring on the buds, but it is a challenge worth accepting. Although tall-growing naturally, *S. tubiflora* can be dwarfed chemically by the use of C.C.C., with flowering thus obtainable on a compact plant only 7 inches tall. Proceed from these species to hybrids with slipper-shaped flowers. You may start these either from seeds or from tubers purchased dormant.

Sinningia regina is one of the most handsome of the species gloxinias. It has velvety olive-green leaves, silver veins, and red undersides. The slipper flowers are slender and dark purple, appearing in generous quantities over an extended season.

S. eumorpha has shiny dark-green leaves and nodding white-slipper flowers marked in the throat with yellow and purple. This one is lovely for itself alone, but also valuable to the hybridizer for it will cross easily with *Rechsteineria* (a closely related gesneriad with tuberous root) and thus produce the intergeneric hybrid *Gloxinera.*

S. pusilla is a true miniature, blooming when it is hardly an inch across. Mature plants seldom reach 2 inches in diameter. Leaves are olive-green with brown veins. Small lavender, slipper flowers are produced the year around. Crosses between this one and *S. eumorpha* produce lovely miniatures with traits of both parents.

Pot *S. pusilla* singly in 2-inch pots or pot several tubers in a small bulb pan. If you can't find a dealer who handles tubers, try them from seed. *S. pusilla* will flower from seed in four months. This little species does not need as much light as larger types, so place it near the end zones of the lights. If leaves begin to yellow on well-fertilized plants, too much light is indicated. This miniature often sets seeds without hand pollination. The tiny pods ripen in a month, often spilling the seed to the soil below. There they form a dense mat of seedlings around the parent. A visitor once asked me if a planter filled with these self-sown plants was a "new kind of flowering ground cover."

There are many lovely slipper-type gloxinias on the market besides the species. Old favorites such as the blue or pink slipper, the newer 'Florence K' with dark-rose-red slippers and foliage quite like S. *regina*, and really spectacular hybrids from Albert Buell, Fischer Greenhouses, Michael Kartuz, and others.

Handsome Hybrid Gloxinias

Hybrid gloxinias with upright facing single and double flowers are among the most breath-taking of all plants. Tubers of the Belgian types with single flowers are available by mail beginning in early November. American-grown doubles are available as started plants or dormant tubers around the year. Single-flowered hybrids from specialists like Albert Buell may be purchased as dormant tubers, started seedlings, or in packets of seeds. I have attained my greatest success with gloxinias by purchasing the tubers, plants, or seeds from mail-order specialists. You will find several listed in chapter 22.

More Miniatures to Come

There are two miniature species gloxinias on the market —*Sinningia pusilla* and S. *concinna*. Breeders are working on hybrid forms. One cross between S. *pusilla* and S. *eumorpha* produced a dainty, lavender-flowered plant with a size midway between the parents. However, it proved to be a disappointment: When the tubers entered dormancy they stayed dormant.

Peggie Schulz, well-known Minneapolis gloxinia specialist and garden writer, has made some successful crosses between miniature S. *pusilla* and gloxineras which produce plants 2 inches wide with 1-inch-long lavender flowers. In the East, Dr. Carl D. Clayberg has been highly successful with similar crosses which have resulted in the outstanding Connecticut Hybrids. Other growers, too, are producing compact gloxinias which can be grown to perfection in 3- and 4-inch pots.

Gloxineras, the Gesneriad "Mules"

Interesting indeed are the gloxineras, and they are easily grown under lights. There are only a few named varieties on the market, but seed is available and from one packet you can get a wide range of colors and forms.

Gloxineras are intergeneric hybrids between *Sinningia eumorpha* and various species of *Rechsteineria;* or between S. *pusilla* and other gloxineras. The first gloxinera to be commerically listed was 'Rosea,' hybridized by Robert Wilson, a specialist in tropical plants, who lives in South Miami, Florida. Parents of this plant were S. *eumorpha* and *Rechsteineria cyclophylla.* Since then many other gloxineras have been named and introduced.

Some gloxineras have as many as three to seven bell-shaped flowers atop each flower stalk. They grow easily under gloxinia culture and are not as subject to bud blast as the larger-flowered gloxinias.

Handsome gloxineras have been produced from crosses between *Sinningia eumorpha* and red-flowered *Rechsteineria cardinalis.* These hybrids have green, heart-shaped leaves covered with soft hair. The tubular flowers (sometimes 2 inches long) are in shades of rose with lavender markings. Outstanding among them is 'Bernice,' a compact, pink-flowered plant, and 'Velvet Charm,' whose dark-rose flower has a lavender throat. A second generation of this group is listed by one dealer as "Harold Hybrids." These have large white flowers with bright-red hairs.

Rechsteineria purpurea, sometimes called triple decker plant, also hybridizes easily with S. *eumorpha* and with some of the gloxineras. R. *purpurea* is a tall plant with a strong central stem producing several whorls of shiny dark-green leaves. Pink flowers dotted and splashed with maroon spring from each whorl of leaves. A handsome hybrid between R. *purpurea* and S. *eumorpha* is presently being propagated for distribution. It has the low flat growth of *eumorpha* and the slender dark leaves of *purpurea.* The flowers are long, tubular, lavender, marked with maroon inside the throat.

In Minneapolis, Mrs. Schulz has produced many hybrid forms using various gloxineras and R. *purpurea* as parents. Among them are tubular lavender flowers on stemless plants. These never stretch and grow tall. Individual flowers stay firm and fresh for three weeks. Other hybrid forms have whorls of velvety leaves so dark they look black. Flowers range from pale shell pink to near red. As yet these plants aren't commercially available, but you can grow your own gloxineras from seed which can be purchased or by making crosses between S. *eumorpha* and the various rechsteinerias.

Gloxinera culture is exactly like that of gloxinias, but these plants usually bloom three or four times a year. Propagate them from leaves or by seed.

13

Gesneriads—Fascinating African Violet Relatives

It took a relative newcomer among the gesneriads to bring attention to the family as a whole. Carl Linnaeus (1707–78) knew about the *Gesneriaceae* and described four genera, but it was not until the African violet (*Saintpaulia*), which had been discovered toward the end of the nineteenth century, rose to popularity some forty years later that interest in the family spread. Today, more than eighty different genera and five hundred species of gesneriads are known. Countless hybrids, chance seedlings, and mutations exist.

As components of a family, these can be described as handsome, often velvety-leaved plants with wheel-shaped, tubular, or bell-shaped flowers, frequently of vivid coloring. So variable are they that a conservatory could be filled with them, and only a taxonomist would be aware that all were members of the same plant family.

The spread of the gesneriads as pot plants in our country has been phenomenal. These plants from the tropical jungles and mountains of Central America, Malaya, Africa, and the mountains of central Bulgaria are practically unique in their ability to adapt to our way of living.

The majority of gesneriads which are suitable for indoor culture grow well in the same soil, temperature range, humidity percentage, and light intensity suggested for African violets (chapter 11). Differences are indicated in the text of this chapter. Some hobbyists enjoy gesneriads as companion plants for African violets. Others grow a few to add variety to lighted gardens of many unrelated plants. Then there are the collectors like me who want to collect, grow, and study as many of these plants as possible.

Gesneriad Growing Habits

There are gesneriads with fibrous roots such as the African violet; gesneriads with potatolike tubers (for example, the gloxinia of florists); and some with scaly rhizomes like those of achimenes.

Most of the fibrous-rooted gesneriads are evergreen, although some of the trailers flower best if given a semidormant period in fall and early winter. At least one of the fibrous-rooted sorts (*Chirita hamosa*) should be treated as an annual. Gesneriads with tubers and scaly rhizomes need a dormant period following the flowering season.

Gesneriads are propagated through cuttings, division, offsets, and by seed (see chapter 7).

Gesneriad Culture under Lights

Gesneriads will grow well in soil recommended for African violets. In combination with a weekly feeding of diluted Ra-Pid-Gro and fish emulsion, applied alternately at half strength, they may be grown in pure vermiculite or sphagnum moss; or in a 50-50 mixture of vermiculite and peat moss. A soil mixture of equal parts garden loam, peat moss, sand (or perlite), and leaf mold (or vermiculite) will also give splendid results with this feeding program.

When in active growth gesneriads need to be watered whenever the topsoil feels dry to the touch. Give them a good watering, from top or bottom, then don't water again until the medium at the surface is dry. When tuberous gesneriads or fibrous-rooted ones such as columnea or hypocyrta are in semidormancy, keep the soil only moist enough to prevent tubers or plant stems from shriveling.

Suitable daytime temperature for most gesneriads ranges from 70 to 75 degrees with a drop of 10 degrees at night. Exceptions to the rule are the hardy or near-hardy genera such as haberlea, jankae, and ramonda. These gesneriads are fine for the alpine garden, for they can stand temperatures to near zero.

Gesneriads will grow with humidity slightly under 40 per cent, but they need at least 50 per cent, and 60 is better for lush growth and full flowering.

Gesneriads are subject to the same pests and ailments which sometimes find their way to African violets. Sterilized soil, well-ventilated, noncrowded growing areas, observing an isolation period before setting newly obtained plants with established ones, and an occasional spraying with an aerosol of houseplant pesticide will give them the needed few ounces of prevention. Should pests or ailments strike, deal with them as suggested in chapter 8.

The Right Light for Gesneriads

Most gesneriads will flower under twelve to sixteen hours of light from a pair of 40-watt fluorescents and a reflector. I've grown them under combinations of one white and one daylight tube; two agricultural lamps such as Gro-Lux or Plant-Gro; one warm white and one daylight; and one natural and one warm white tube. All have been satisfactory. The main thing is getting the plants close enough to the lights. No hard and fast rules can be laid down for these plants because they vary in size from tiny flat-growing 2-inch gloxinera 'Petite' to 18-inch rechsteinerias and smithianthas.

Gesneriads for Beginners

It has been my pleasure to open many boxes of plants, but I still recall vividly my first collection of episcias which arrived by mail from Miami's Fantastic Gardens. Soon I was indescribably proud of the way those tropical beauties thrived in my greenhouse and window garden. In the years since, I have seen episcias grow even more beautifully in fluorescent-lighted gardens. When these plants are given reasonably satisfactory conditions they will grow foliage that is unrivaled in luxuriant beauty, and when the temperatures are warm, the humidity high, and the light constant they will put on a breath-taking flower show.

I suspect that these plants would have continued to be rare if an enterprising grower had not christened one of them a "Flame Violet," and promoted it widely as a trailing violet with scarlet flowers. Since the African violet is no violet itself, and the episcia is not a saintpaulia, only related to it, it is farfetched indeed to call it "Flame Violet." There are two common names heard occasionally that seem much more acceptable to me. One is peacock foliage plant, for truly the leaves do bear some of the iridescent colors from this handsome bird, and the other is heavenly strawberry, a pleasing reference to the plant's habit of sending out stolons or runners like a strawberry. There are several accepted pronunciations for the name, but the one generally considered proper is epi-SEE-ah.

As recently as ten years ago there were less than two dozen named episcias in commerce. Today there are more than a hundred varieties named and registered with the American Gloxinia Society, and the future promises many more. Primarily these are foliage plants, sometimes compared with the more ubiquitous coleus because every seed-pod holds a potential myriad of new foliage colors and variations. The flowers, a secondary reason for growing episcias, have five lobes with a noticeable tube. They range in size from the diameter of a quarter up to a silver dollar, and the colors include lilac, blue, red, scarlet, white, and yellow. Foliage may be green, all the way from a light lettuce color to a dark jade; or bronze to copper; or a silvery to purplish rosy pink. The foliage of some varieties is hairy, that of others is smooth or glossy.

The catalogs of most houseplant specialists offer a good selection of named episcias. You may find them also at local greenhouses, especially where African violets are sold. Northern growers will ship episcias only during warm weather.

Episcias need tropical warmth, a range of 65 to 85 degrees being nearly ideal during the winter months. A temperature of 50 degrees, or lower, will cause them to collapse as if frosted. If this happens, move the plants to warmth, high humidity, and good light. Usually they will recover from a chill.

Episcias are ideal for fluorescent-light culture. A setup that grows African violets will turn out nearly perfect episcias. Growers once recommended that episcias be situated toward the ends of the fixture, with violets in between. Now we know that the more light the plants receive the better they will flower.

The easiest way to propagate episcias is to remove vigorous stolons and insert the stems in moist peat moss and vermiculite. In a warm, humid atmosphere they will root in a few days. Episcia seeds are tiny, though not as small as African violets, and need to be sown on top of a fine, sterile medium such as screened sphagnum moss, and kept constantly moist and warm. Keep in bright light and transplant when large enough to handle.

Episcias are one of the most beautiful of all hanging basket plants. They can be enjoyed in a flowerpot hung up with wire or string, or you can go lavish and fill a wire or redwood basket with rooted cuttings. Soon the stolons will create a cascade of foliage, set also with many flowers if the atmosphere is warm, humid, and bright. Since a long cascade of stolons is hard to accommodate in a lighted garden, I prefer to let episcias spread out instead of down. You can also grow them as specimen plants. To do this, pinch out all of the stolons when they are still small. This causes the main plant to grow larger leaves, and in ample light, warmth, and high humidity, the flower crop will be unusually heavy, foiled by a plant of unusually handsome foliage.

The rechsteinerias are tuberous-rooted plants that are easily grown with a culture like that for gloxinias (see chapter 12). *R. cyclophylla* has shiny green leaves and bears showers of small, red, tubular flowers. *R. cardinalis* has furry, heart-shaped, emerald-green leaves and long, bright-red flowers.

Kohleria, smithiantha, and achimenes grow from scaly rhizomes. Plant one or two kohleria or smithiantha rhizomes to a 4-inch pot of African violet soil. Plant four or five achimenes rhizomes to a 5- or 6-inch pot of soil. Give the rhizomes a light covering of soil, then water. Start at room temperature. Gentle bottom heat will speed growth, but it is not necessary. Plant kohleria and smithiantha any time of the year; achimenes from January to April.

You can root budded achimenes tips and have them in flower all year. Or, after the rhizomes have been dormant six to eight weeks in autumn, repot and try to force into winter bloom. For this treatment, Michael Kartuz, writing in *The Gloxinian,* suggests early-blooming varieties such as achimenes 'Ambroise Verschaffelt,' 'Purple King,' 'Camille Brozzoni,' *A. ehrenbergii,* or 'Little Beauty.'

All of these gesneriads that grow from scaly rhizomes are easy to grow under lights. Keep the plants close to the tubes when they are in new growth. As stems lengthen, move them away from the tubes. They usually flower at 10 to 11 inches from the tubes with sixteen light hours per day. When mature plants stop flowering, gradually dry them off. Remove rhizomes from the pots and store dry in vermiculite or perlite in a frost-free place.

Kohleria amabilis has furry green leaves with attractive brown markings. Its tubular rose flowers are dotted inside with purple. Flowers last up to six weeks. *K. lindeniana* has smaller green leaves of olive green, prominently silver-veined, and pale violet and white flowers that are fragrant.

There is a wide choice in achimenes. You will find varieties in shades of pink, blue, lavender, purple, red, and yellow. Most have single flowers, but a series of double-flowered achimenes has recently been introduced.

Smithiantha, sometimes listed as temple bells, and long ago known as *Naegelia,* has velvety foliage and tubular flowers. *S. cinnabarina* has glowing garnet-red leaves and reddish-orange flowers. *S. zebrina* leaves are green marbled with red; the flowers are red with yellow spots. Hybridizers have been at work with smithianthas, and from Cornell University a new series ranging in color from near white 'Abbey' to poppy-red 'Vespers' has come. As my manuscript went into final typing, word came from Pat Antonelli of Antonelli Brothers, Santa Cruz, California, that his firm will introduce in 1965 a series of outstanding smithiantha hybrids.

Streptocarpus, with wrinkled, straplike leaves and large, exotic white, pink, or purple, tubular flowers, grow beautifully under the same culture recommended for African violets. Propagate through leaves, division, or by seed.

There are many columneas, but *C. tulae* var. *flava,* a small-leaved yellow-flowered trailer, is easiest to flower under lights. This fibrous-rooted plant thrives in living-room temperatures with fourteen to sixteen hours of artificial light daily. Propagate from tip cuttings or seed.

If you enjoy growing plants from seed, try *Chirita hamosa.* Its oval leaves are bright yellow-green; flowers, small

Figure 5. Smithiantha multiflora, a hybrid form of temple bells, and one of the most beautiful of all gesneriads to grow under lights.

and tubular, are white and blue. Treat this gesneriad as an annual, that is, discard it after the initial flowering season.

Gesneriads for Advanced Growers

After you succeed with the more common of these unusual gesneriads, you will enjoy some of the newer varieties of episcias. These aren't necessarily more difficult to handle than the other kinds, but they are more expensive and beginners often hesitate to practice on them.

Episcia 'Shimmer' has leaves of chocolate green with silvery green overlay, and scarlet flowers. 'Silver Lining' has brown leaves covered with silvery lines, and small orange flowers.

Episcia dianthiflora isn't new or expensive, yet it takes a skillful grower to bring it into full bloom. Leaves are small and green; flowers are white, dotted inside with purple and the margins are deeply fringed.

Hypocyrta nummularia, a trailer with small, rounded leaves and red, pouchlike flowers, can be a challenge to under-light gardeners. Rest it in the winter, keeping the soil just moist enough so that the stems do not shrivel. Propagate from stem cuttings. *H. wettsteini* is a neat plant with small, glossy, near-black leaves and orange-pouched flowers. It is a rare collector's item.

Petrocosmea kerri, with velvety green leaves and white flowers marked with a bright orange-yellow eye, is closely related to saintpaulia—but not close enough so that the two can be hybridized. Petrocosmea needs more water than African violets, but it will grow in the same type of soil or one which is considerably heavier. It seldom flowers freely under lights, but you may just be the one who discovers what it needs to make it flower as freely as violets do.

Aeschynanthus or lipstick plant (formerly known as trichosporum) is a trailer, often seen in hanging baskets. Its leaves are waxy; the tubular flowers are red or orange. Plants can be grown under African violet culture or potted in coarse sphagnum moss or firbark and given weekly feedings of diluted fertilizer. *A. marmoratus* has mottled green leaves, green and orange flowers; *A. speciosus,* often a show winner, has flowers of orange and red, growing to 4 inches long.

Chinese chirita, *C. sinensis,* is a low-growing plant with

slender bright-green leaves vividly patterned with silver. Its small flowers are pale lilac. Fibrous-rooted, it grows with African violet culture.

Gesneriads for Collectors

Collector's items are seldom easily obtained, so some of the gesneriads mentioned here will have to be grown from seed. Some are obtainable from specialized dealers, but the price may be high.

Alloplectus vittatus has velvety green leaves with silvery gray veins. The pouched yellow flowers are in bright-red calyxes. This evergreen gesneriad responds to African violet culture, but it revels in tropical warmth and high humidity.

If you like small plants, grow *Chirita micromusa*. It will bloom from seed in four months, flowering when it is but 2 inches high. The smooth, bright-yellow flowers are borne above interesting pale-green leaves. One large, oval leaf backed by a pair of small, pointed leaves, characterizes this little chirita. African violet culture suits it. If larger plants are your preference, *Chirita asperifolia* will enhance your lighted garden. It is a bushy plant with tubular purple and white flowers.

You may also like to try some of the college-bred columneas, recently introduced from Cornell University. Dwarf, compact 'Campus Queen' has red flowers in feathery calyxes and 'Cayugan' is an upright grower with 3-inch orange flowers. Specialists list a number of other columnea hybrids; especially those that grow upright are suited to under-light gardens.

Episcia melittifolia, an upright grower with square stem and magenta flowers, doesn't send out stolons. It grows readily in any light soil. I have one plant that thrives in perlite with weekly feedings of soluble fertilizer. It compares favorably with others growing in regular soil. I believe this one could be grown with only ten to twelve hours of light daily. It sets seed easily, with the pods maturing in four to six weeks.

Consider the diastemas too. They grow from scaly rhizomes and form plants of thin or velvety green leaves and produce a great array of small white flowers dotted with pink or purple. One dealer lists an undetermined species with blue flowers described as "An interesting plant for low-light levels."

Last, but not least, I think of nautilocalyx, a handsome foliage plant with inconspicuous straw-colored flowers. I find two of the species attractive and recommend them for every lighted garden: *N. forgeti*, with wavy-edged, glossy green leaves patterned red-brown, and *N. lynchi*, with shiny, dark, purple-red leaves. When these plants begin to age, and the stems grow too tall, make tip cuttings. Soon you will again have vigorous new plants in the right proportions for a lighted garden.

14

Begonias for All-Year Interest

If you are among the legion of gardeners who enjoy collecting begonias, your pleasures will be doubled when you start growing them under fluorescent lights. This vast plant family has species and varieties to please everyone. There are miniatures such as ruby-and-silver rex 'Baby Rainbow,' 12-inch 'Fleecealba,' with furry white leaves and sprays of white flowers, jewel-toned rexes, exquisitely flowered tuberous types, the ever-blooming semperflorens, and hundreds more. Best of all, you can grow them to perfection in a fluorescent-lighted garden.

Lighted Growing Areas for Begonias

Since most begonias do not need full sun, they are ideal subjects for growing under artificial light. Any of the setups mentioned in chapters 3 and 4 will suit them. If you grow your plants in a greenhouse you will find suggestions for lighted space-stretchers in chapter 20. Your choice of light setups will be decided by your space for lights and the type of begonias you enjoy growing. When you don't have to reckon with growing your plants at windows, you will discover many nooks large enough to accommodate a pair of 40-watt lights. (After all, these units are only 48 inches long.) If your budget is limited, start with a pair of standard-type fluorescents, one tube warm white and one daylight, or one natural and one daylight. Suspend the tubes and a 15-inch reflector over a 2 × 4 foot table or counter and you'll have enough light to grow thirty begonias in 3-inch pots, or dozens of seedlings or cuttings in smaller pots. If yours is a collection of short and tall begonias, suspend the lights with pulleys so you can adjust them to fit the tallest plants. Boost the short ones up to the light with inverted flowerpots.

If your budget will stretch to allow the purchase of a four-tube fixture, this will be even better, for with the increased light you can grow a magnificent crop of tuberous begonias, or handle successfully a group of small angelwing begonias, or collector's items such as finger-leaved white-flowered 'Lady Clare,' red, green, and white 'Richland,' and pink-bearded 'Vesperia.'

Setups such as these are generally relegated to basements, attics, even bedrooms. But you can grow begonias, and especially the lower-growing types, in any of the decorative units described in chapter 4.

Rex begonias, particularly, are a rainbow of color when viewed under the lavender agricultural lamps. A lighted glass case of them in the living room or foyer is as handsome as a jeweler's case of precious gems. Under these special lights the red, pink, and purple bands or markings deepen and glow.

In a living-room case I often alternate pots of 'Joe Hayden' with its near-black and red leaves with African violet 'White Orchid,' or one of the double pink violets. In this case both begonias and violets grow in squatty 4-inch pots 11 inches from 40-watt tubes.

I have never found an easier plant for growing under lights than the beautifully patterned *B. masoniana,* sometimes listed as 'Iron Cross.' This one has hairy, pebbled, moss-green leaves centered with a wine-colored replica of an iron cross. When I'm not growing it with other begonias,

I like to use it as a companion plant for wine-red streptocarpus or African violets.

Growing the smaller begonias under lights presents no problem, for they grow under setups spaced exactly as those for African violets, that is, with a distance of 18 inches between the light tubes and the growing surface. However, taller types, which may have to be grown under light fixtures suspended on pulleys, often grow so tall they reach the light tubes. If you have no greenhouse to which these begonias can graduate, nip out the top of the plant as it nears the light tube. This won't harm the plant, and it usually makes the lower parts bushier. You can always root the tips for additional plants.

The ever-blooming semperflorens or wax begonias are just that when grown under lights. They grow and flower under any combination of white fluorescents—daylight, natural, or warm white. If you like the double-flowered kinds, grow a complete garden of them under any of your fluorescent setups. They'll bloom steadily. But if you grow them under the agricultural lamps, the red and pink flower balls will shine like Christmas-tree ornaments.

Time Schedule for Begonias

Burn the lights for fourteen to sixteen hours if you are growing begonias only; if you grow begonias and African violets or some of the other gesneriads, give them twelve to sixteen hours daily. (Violets tend to bleach under too much light.) You will soon discover which of your begonias, too, can be grown with less light. 'Iron Cross' (*B. masoniana*) for instance, is one which thrives with twelve to thirteen hours of artificial light daily. Summer-flowering tuberous begonias, known as long-day plants, require at least fourteen hours of light daily.

Begonia Culture under Lights

If your garden soil grows fine tuberous begonias, use two parts of it to one part peat moss for your indoor begonias. Otherwise, make a mixture of equal parts garden loam, sand (or perlite), peat moss, and leaf mold (or vermiculite).

I like to grow the majority of my begonias in 3- and 4-inch pots, but I realize that older, larger plants must be shifted to larger containers.

Begonias are classified as fibrous-rooted, rhizomatous, tuberous, and semituberous.

B. semperflorens is fibrous-rooted; *B. rex, B. heracleifolia,* and *B. ricinifolia* are among the rhizomatous types; *B. tuberhybrida* is our summer-flowering tuberous begonia; *B. socotrana* and its many varieties, called semituberous, are the Christmas begonias, and these are also short-day plants that require special treatment for full success.

Daytime temperatures of 70 to 75 degrees, with a drop of 10 degrees for nighttime, are suitable for begonias. They will thrive in 40 to 60 per cent humidity. Raise moisture content in the air by any of the methods suggested in chapter 5.

Water begonias in active growth when the surface soil is dry to the touch. Don't let the soil be dripping wet for more than a few hours or rot may result.

Begonias in active growth need to be fed regularly. I alternate biweekly feedings of a chemical fertilizer such as Ra-Pid-Gro with those of an organic such as Atlas Fish Emulsion. Do not fertilize newly potted or dormant begonias.

Tuberous begonias need to be dried off and rested during the winter. Rhizomatous begonias enter a semidormant period in fall or around Christmastime. Leaves of some kinds even drop and plants stop growing. When this happens stop fertilizing and water sparingly. They can be moved from the lights during the resting period, but should never be stored in a completely dark place. When growth shows, resume watering, fertilizing, and normal lighting. Rhizomatous begonias need winter light if they are to give a bumper crop of flowers.

Propagating Begonias

Begonias are easily grown from seed. The seeds are fine as dust and may be started by following the methods suggested for planting such seed in chapter 7. You can buy seed, make your plants produce their own seed, or purchase ready-seeded planting units.

Both male and female flowers are found on the same begonia plants. The female flower always has a winged ovary directly under the petals. The male blossom is usually larger and has a pollen-filled center. To make your plant produce seed, simply remove some of the yellow pollen from a male flower, place it on the tip of the corkscrew-like yellow pistil in the female plant. If the pollination is successful, seeds will form and ripen within six weeks. Seedlings of B. semperflorens will flower in four to six months when grown under lights at suggested temperatures. Most other types take up to a year to flower. However, you can have a marvelous summer display of tuberous begonias from seed if you start the seed in January.

Most begonias are easily rooted from cuttings, but especially the wax types. Cuttings taken from new basal shoots give nicer plants. I have had them bloom under lights when they were 2 inches high. Stem and foliage color of light-grown semperflorens is not as ruddy as on those grown in sunshine, but this doesn't bother me when the plants send out such an abundance of bloom.

To propagate the variegated leaved calla-lily begonia,

also a wax or semperflorens type, take a cutting with some green in it. This type roots easily under lights. Once rooted and transplanted, calla-lily begonias need to be kept cooler and drier than other semperflorens. A few inches directly beneath the tubes in the center of a lighted garden, a calla-lily begonia can be brought to show-winning excellence.

Stem cuttings and root divisions of angel-wing begonias grow readily under lights, but the mature plants may get too tall for ease of light culture. The recent hybrids from Belva Kusler, introduced by Tropical Paradise, are an exception. They tend to be low-growing and ever-blooming. I recommend them wholeheartedly for fluorescent culture. Varieties include 'Anna Christine' (red), 'Gigi Fleetham' (white, flushed pink), 'Jeanne Fleetham' (white), 'Laura Engelbert' (red), 'Lenore Olivier' (fragrant salmon-pink), and 'Sophie Cecile' (rose-pink).

Propagate hairy-leaved begonias such as red-whiskered *B. scharffiana,* silver and green *B. metallica,* and others in this group with leaf or stem cuttings. Likewise, all the many-hued rexes. These obliging plants are so easily propagated you can even divide their leaves into wedges, each with a main vein, and root them (see chapter 7).

If you fancy single-stemmed tuberous begonias for your outdoor garden, remove the extra stems from spring-started tubers, stick them in your favorite rooting medium, set them under lights, as close as you can get them to the tubes without withering the leaves. They will flower with fourteen hours of light per day. However, in my experience, they seldom form tubers of sufficient size to keep over for another year. You can also propagate tuberous begonias through tuber division, leaving a sprout to each piece of tuber. Dust cut surfaces with sulfur or Fermate before planting.

If fall frost threatens budded garden-grown tuberous begonias, dig and pot them, removing all shoots that have finished flowering. Harden them off a few days on a sunny porch or other sheltered area. Then bring into the fluorescent-lighted garden for several weeks more enjoyment of the satiny flowers.

Another way to handle frost-threatened tuberous begonias is to break off healthy tip growth, making cuttings about 4 inches long. Take these to your fluorescent-lighted garden and root in moist vermiculite, or perlite. Transplant to 4-inch pots of regular begonia soil. By midwinter these will be full of bloom, provided they have at least fourteen hours of light daily; the use of at least one plant-growth lamp such as Gro-Lux is recommended in order to have satisfactory off-season bloom of tuberous begonias.

Begonia Pests and Diseases

Lacking good culture, begonias are subject to just about every kind of pest and disease which troubles growing plants: aphids, black and white flies, mealybugs, cyclamen and red spider mites, nematodes, scale and thrips. Ailments include bud drop, mildew, leaf and stem rot. But never let a list of such possible annoyances keep you from growing any favorite plants, and especially begonias. I mention troubles merely because they can happen when plants and people don't "see" eye-to-eye on culture.

In all the years I have grown begonias, I have never found insects other than a few thrips on them, and although they (rexes in particular) may rot, they are so easily propagated that I always have a few spare leaves down so new plants can take the place of those lost.

Begonias for Foliage Beauty

The begonia clan has such a wealth of beautifully colored, patterned, and shaped foliage that it is possible to assemble a foliage garden of great beauty for your under-light gardens. And as a bonus, all of these fine-foliaged plants also flower in season.

Begonia rex has been so highly hybridized it is difficult to give accurate descriptions of the many varieties. The best way to choose these exquisite plants is to browse in a greenhouse and select colors and forms you find most allur-ing. Be assured that all of them will grow under lights. Sev-eral mail-order specialists list named varieties. Here are a few I like, many of which are older varieties, but easily grown. The coloring refers only to the leaves. Flowers are either near white or soft pink.

REX BEGONIAS FOR BEGINNERS
    'Helen Teupel' silver and maroon
    'Lavender Glow' blend of orchid and purple
    'Peter Pan' silver and green
    'Curly Silver Sweet' ruffled silver, red veins
    'Merry Christmas' red and green
    'Red Berry' miniature, shining wine-red
    'Mulberry' reddish-purple and silver

REX BEGONIAS FOR COLLECTORS
    'Avila' rose, silver, and green
    'Curly Fire Flush' spiral form, green and red
    'Her Majesty' dark purple and pink
    'Mohegan' rose with near-black border
    'Perle de Paris' silver-green, yellow flowers
    'Prince Charming' green dotted with silver, flushed pink

Other rhizomatous begonias have leaves of intricate form and pattern. Flowers are pink or white. The first half dozen are easy to grow and readily available from most specialists. The second group is rarer, sometimes more expensive, but not necessarily any more difficult to grow under lights.

Six Rhizomatous Begonias for a Beginner
'Black Shadows' small green, star-shaped leaves, black stitching at edges
'Beatrice Haddrell' near-black, star-shaped leaves, light-green veins
'Ricky Minter' bronze and dark green, frilled and crested
kenworthyi five-lobed, greenish-red
'Stitched Leaf' round green leaves, stitched black edges
'Sylvan Rhapsody' oval, dark-green leaves, red undersides

Six Rhizomatous Begonias for a Collector
'Bright Eyes' black-green star-shaped leaves, perfumed pink flowers
conchaefolia shell-shaped, green, succulent leaves
'Dark Sheen' small, angled green leaves, dark margins
decora velvety brown leaves, fragrant white flowers
'Illsley' dark-green miniature with stitched edges
'Eloise' small, dark-green leaves

15

Orchids Every Day the Fluorescent Way

Probably no common flower is as surrounded by confusing mystique about culture as the orchid. It was an article in the October, 1957, issue of *Flower and Garden* magazine that led me into the wonderful adventure of growing my own orchids. Dr. Aphrodite J. Hofsommer of Webster Groves, Missouri, wrote that she was growing orchids—and very successfully too—in what had once been a coalbin in the basement of her home. Fluorescent lights were the answer, of course. Later I had the pleasure of visiting the Drs. Hofsommer—Aphrodite and Armin (Jack)—and seeing for myself that a refurbished coalbin with flat-white, rubber-based paint slathered over walls and ceiling, and the addition of fluorescent-lighted benches, had indeed transformed a useless, dreary basement room into a veritable orchid-arium.

The Hofsommer coalbin, known today as the "Green Thumb Room" by thousands of persons who have read Dr. Aphrodite's monthly column in the *Bulletin* of the American Orchid Society in 1962 and 1963, measures 9 × 11 feet. Double-decker benches along three walls provide an amazing amount of growing space in this small room. Benches are lighted by batteries of four-tube, 48-inch fixtures, each containing one daylight and one Sylvania deluxe cool white and two Gro-Lux lamps, thirty-six tubes in all. At last report the Hofsommers' tests revealed that Gro-Lux tubes alone were not the answer to orchid flowering. Three-inch-deep pans of wet gravel cover the surface of each bench. These are spanned by expanded metal racks or shelves from old refrigerators, and the orchid pot bases rest on these—near enough to benefit from moisture that rises from the gravel, but not resting on it where water-logging of the roots could result.

The Hofsommers exercise their trained, analytical minds constantly in making the "Green Thumb Room" a better place for orchids. One recent report tells of running an exhaust fan from about 11 A.M. every day until the lights go on at night. This comes on at about the time the orchids are watered or sprayed. It is placed 18 inches above the floor facing the ceiling between benches. As the fan circulates air from the damp floor and moistened foliage, humidity increases as much as 10 per cent in the first hour.

A typical winter flower report from the Hofsommers, in the American Orchid Society *Bulletin*, goes like this, "We have in bloom a *Cycnoches chlorochilon*, two *Dendrobium phalaenopsis*, one *Phalaenopsis* 'Grace Palm,' a *Cattleya skinneri*, two *Cattleya* hybrids, one a yellow *Lc.* 'Mimi Koehler.' In bud are ten *Cattleya* hybrids, two of them *Brassocattleyas*, and three *Cymbidiums*, one a white *Cym.* Alexanderi 'Perfection' and two Dos Pueblos crosses." During warm weather, most of the Hofsommer collection is placed outdoors, formerly on tables in partial shade, others suspended from tree branches and frames. Now a plastic-roofed screen house is used. Cool-loving cymbidiums are placed near a birdbath where water splashed on the pots transpires in summer heat, thus lowering the temperature of the growing medium and roots. Drainage here is accomplished by elevation on a couple of bricks.

Are You Ready for Orchids?

If you have been reasonably successful in growing other potted plants such as African violets and begonias, I would suggest that you are ready for orchids. Start by sending for the catalogs of mail-order specialists in orchids (see chapter 22). Study the literature you receive. If you are serious in your intent to grow orchids well in a fluorescent-lighted garden, join the American Orchid Society so that you will receive the monthly *Bulletin*. You may request a list of the Society's publications for the beginner and for those growing orchids without a greenhouse. A bibliography is also available. Or you may write directly to Dr. Hofsommer for reprints of her articles in the *Bulletin*, and a report of her address before the Third World Orchid Congress in London, 1960. For complete information about membership, contact the Society in care of the Botanical Museum of Harvard University, Cambridge, Massachusetts 02138.

When you are ready to invest some money in orchid plants, start with mature, blooming-size specimens. Do not spend your budget on seedlings or half-grown plants; save this kind of buying for when you have become an experienced collector. The mere mention of the word "orchid" brings to mind for most of us a frilly, large Cattleya hybrid. You may want to specialize in cattleyas, but remember, there are literally thousands of other orchids from which to choose. Start with a dozen inexpensive botanical types, or older hybrids. Later you will be ready to indulge in a prize hybrid with a devastating pricetag.

Some orchids are more adaptable to under-light, home culture, than others. Catalogs often make helpful suggestions about the kinds most likely to succeed under the care of an amateur. As a beginner, I learned the hard way that some of the less spectacular botanical or natural species orchids, incidentally less expensive also than many of the cultivated hybrids, got along better with me than the others. I achieved my first real success with orchids while doing research for my earlier book, *Miniature Plants for Home and Greenhouse*. The silver orchid became my favorite of the twenty-five kinds I grew in those days. It is known botanically as *Erythroides nobilis argyrocentrus*, and is one of the few orchids I have grown that actually thrives in a closed terrarium where humidity is constantly high. Soggy osmunda fiber or bark are not to its liking, of course. For light culture, this orchid is truly superb.

Other miniature orchids I recommend highly for underlight gardens include *Aerides japonicum, Cattleya aclandiae, C. luteola* and *C. walkeriana, Lockhartia oersderii* and *L. pallida, Mystacidium distichum, Oncidium triquetrum, Paphiopedilum concolor, P. fairieanum* and *P. bellatulum,* and *Rodriguezia fragrans.*

Branching out to other orchids of larger size, here are ten that I can recommend for fluorescent-light culture from personal experience: *Brassavola nodosa, Cattleya skinneri, Cycnoches chlorochilon, Epidendrum cochleatum, Lycaste aromatica, Odontoglossum grande, Oncidium sarcodes, Paphiopedilum maudiae,* and *Stanhopea oculata.*

Another grower who has been unusually successful in growing orchids by means of fluorescent lights in a basement garden was kind enough to share his list with me. It includes *Cattleya citrinia, C. gaskelliana, C. guttata, C. harrisoniana, C. luteola, C. skinneri,* and *C.* 'St. Louis,' *Cycnoches chlorochilon,* cypripediums (known botanically as paphiopedilums), *Mormodes igneum, Odontoglossum grande,* oncidiums, *Sophronotis grandiflora, Vanda rothschildiana* seedlings, and *Zygopetalum wendlandii.*

How to Grow Orchids the Fluorescent Way

Before I give some brief guidelines for growing orchids by means of phytoillumination, I would like to bring your attention to two relatively new methods prevalent in the orchid world. For one thing, we have been presuming for years that orchids needed the incubatorlike conditions of a Wardian case, that is, an air-tight glass-covered box. This is not only unnecessary but even a hindrance to most orchids you will be likely to attempt. What orchids do need is a buoyant, moist atmosphere that is well charged with fresh air. Also, there has been considerable confusion about the orchid-growing medium. Those that are epiphytes were grown almost entirely in osmunda fiber (from the root of a fern). This tough material was difficult for many amateurs to use, both at potting time and later in keeping it properly moist. Today, shredded firbark is in wide use for epiphytic orchids, and it is much more easily handled in all phases of culture than osmunda. The terrestrial orchids are cultivated in various kinds of growing mediums. These may include parts of garden loam, peat moss, shredded bark, sphagnum moss, or osmunda fiber. Since different genera and species require variations in the amounts of these ingredients, no recipe is given here. Orchid catalogs usually provide this kind of information, and if not, it should come in a cultural sheet with your order.

Orchids vary so widely in cultural requirements that it is nearly impossible to lay down specific rules unless they are applied directly to one kind of orchid. My suggestions here are intended as broad generalities to give you an idea of what orchids will need in your fluorescent-lighted garden. Further reading about any one of them may reveal that the plant needs more coolness than the average I've given; or more hours of light. But these are variables you can control.

Light Setups for Orchids

While the usual fluorescent fixture with two 40-watt tubes may be ample for lighting the paphiopedilums, and some miniature orchids, most successful growers today recommend fixtures with at least three tubes, and preferably four. Reports in the American Orchid Society *Bulletin* indicate that growers use as little as nine and a half hours of light daily, up to eighteen and twenty for seedlings, but most seem to prefer thirteen and a half to fourteen hours illumination out of every twenty-four. The Hofsommers use thirteen and a half hours daily except twelve in December and January. This promotes flowering of the light-controlled group of *Cattleya labiata* hybrids. Also, there should be 10 per cent total wattage provided by incandescent bulbs placed anywhere in the room, but not close enough to burn the orchid leaves.

Humidity is vital for success with orchids. The minimum is 40 per cent, but 60 to 70 per cent is a better range. This needs to be combined with a reasonable amount of fresh air provided indirectly so that it does not strike the plants in a cold or hot draft. In a basement plant room, a small circulating fan may be used. Many growers run a cool-vapor humidifier to increase humidity, with a small circulating fan directed on the mist as it comes from the humidifier. Do not direct circulating fans on plants, however, as this tends to dry out foliage and flower buds. It is understood, of course, that you will fill waterproof galvanized metal or plastic trays with pebbles and water, then put wire or redwood racks on top on which to set the orchid pots from the outset. Watering should be done before midday if possible, as wet leaves at night encourage fungus growth.

Temperature for orchids is easily provided, unless you choose types noted to be very cool growers. A great number of orchids thrive in temperatures that are comfortable for human beings—specifically a range of 55 to 60 degrees at night, with a rise of as much as 10 to 15 degrees by day. The nightly drop in temperature promotes bud development.

Water the growing medium well from the top, and only if it is dry. One way to determine this is to lift the pot. If it feels light, add tepid water. If it is heavy, don't. Practically every orchid grower has to develop his own ability to judge when each orchid needs watering. Some say they mist the foliage once or twice daily, but add water to the growing medium only about once a week. Fertilizing, too, is subject to many variations depending on each plant and time of year. I maintain a weekly feeding plan, using very diluted water-solubles such as Ra-Pid-Gro (chemical) and Atlas Fish Emulsion (organic) at approximately one-fourth the usual strength. Fertilizer is withheld from plants immediately after they finish flowering until new growth becomes apparent.

Repotting and dividing are best done at the beginning of an active growing season. For most orchids, spring is a good time.

Failure with orchids is most often attributable to over-watering, lack of moisture in the air around the plants, and insufficient lighting. Orchids really are easy to grow as under-light plants, that is, if you do your part in knowing and providing the few simple requirements. In fact, practically any successful home orchid grower will tell you they are vastly easier to grow than African violets. This kind of reasoning is something like an American and Frenchman debating which language is more easily spoken. It's what we are accustomed to that counts.

16

Geraniums for Lots of Color

If your geranium collection has outgrown your window
space; if lack of natural light keeps your geraniums from
flowering during the winter months; if you'd like to grow
an abundance of geraniums for bedding out in the spring;
or if you would like to carry on a geranium hybridizing
program, consider growing the plants under artificial light.
Even these proven sun worshippers can be successfully
handled under lights, giving a year-round display of colorful, sometimes fragrant, foliage and bright blooms.

Light Requirements of Geraniums

Geraniums need full sun for good growth and flowering.
During the long days of winter it is difficult to give them all
the natural light they need. If you are making light setups
with geraniums in mind, consider using three or four 40-
watt tubes or supplementing a pair of 40-watt tubes with
10 per cent incandescent light. The fluorescent lamps can
be combinations of cool white and daylight; daylight and
natural; one of the special agricultural lamps and one natural fluorescent; or all agricultural lamps. If your collection
is large, you might like to grow them under the 74-watt,
96-inch tubes. Burn the lights from fourteen to sixteen hours
each day.

When it isn't feasible to provide specially lighted quarters for geraniums, supplement the window light with fluorescent light or combine it with the light from a 60-watt incandescent. Leave the lights on during the entire day and a few hours at night, just long enough to give them the equivalent of twelve to sixteen hours of artificial light.

Relegate large, old plants to basement setups where they can grow luxuriantly under lights. Unless you have lights on pulleys or chains it is difficult to accommodate the large kinds. Keep upstairs lighting for choice varieties, perhaps some of the scenteds, variegated-leaved types, dwarfs, and cuttings you have brought in from the garden.

If you have never grown geraniums under lights, you will have to do some experimenting before you discover the distances between the plant and the tube which suit your geraniums best.

In a planter case with a pair of 40-watt tubes, one natural and one agricultural lamp, I have a dozen geraniums in 3-inch ceramic pots. They have grown in this case under normal living-room temperatures for five months. Pink- and white-flowered ones produced the most bloom. 'Genie Irene,' with shocking-pink flowers is so stunning under the rays of the lavender-tinted agricultural lamp, I am thinking of growing several more plants of it along with the golden-leaved 'Cloth of Gold' in this case. These light tubes are 11 inches from the plant shelf, with the tops of some plants only 2 inches from the lights. Others, such as miniatures 'Tiny Tim,' 'Little Gem,' and 'Mischief,' are 6 inches from the lights. All show remarkably bushy growth.

A light spraying with Gibberellic acid (available in convenient aerosol form) applied as geranium buds are first showing color increases the size of some varieties and makes them last longer. This is particularly true with double-flowered whites. It also keeps the double whites from showing browned centers a few days after opening.

Countertop collection of gesneriads, featuring gloxinera 'Velvet Charm' front and center. Plant of columnea is visible to the left. African violet 'Excitement,' whose foliage sometimes becomes nearly half white with variegation, shows at right, next to an episcia. (SELECT STUDIOS)

Small-growing achimenes 'Coral Gem,' a new double from the Park Seed Company, is excellent for under-light culture.

Hybrid streptocarpus from Antonelli Brothers; flowers clear blue with white throat, leaves rich, dark green. (VESTER DICK)

Collection of begonias in fluorescent-lighted case; left to right: 'Fleece-alba,' *masoniana*, a rex hybrid, three double-flowered semperflorens, another rex hybrid, and a single-flowered semperflorens. (SELECT STUDIOS)

Rhizomatous begonia 'Cleopatra' grows beautifully under lights. (BRILMAYER)

Phalaenopsis orchid 'Ruby Lips' from Alberts & Merkel Brothers.

Dwarf-growing orchid *Dendrobium kentrophyllum*, also from Alberts & Merkel, makes an unusual specimen for under-light culture.

Orchids thriving under lights in basement area that was once a coal bin in the Webster Groves, Missouri, home of Dr. Aphrodite J. Hofsommer.

Collection of geraniums in lighted countertop garden. There are scenteds, ivy-leafs, fancy-leafs, and hortorums, and a plant of dwarf citrus for variety, fragrance, and fruit. (SELECT STUDIOS)

Pelargonium hortorum 'Lady Luck' is a small-growing zonal geranium with dark red double flowers. (MERRY GARDENS)

Geranium Culture under Lights

Ideally, geraniums need to be grown in daytime temperatures of 70 to 75 degrees with a nighttime drop of 10 to 5 degrees. Professional growers would hasten to add, "except for late propagations, which may be grown somewhat warmer." Since most of us grow our geraniums for pleasure rather than profit, we can handle them in temperatures suited to most other flowering houseplants, dropping the night temperature 5 to 10 degrees.

Geraniums grow well in any good friable garden loam, but I find they handle best in pots when I grow them in a firm mixture such as three parts of soil, two parts peat moss, and one part sand (or perlite).

Geraniums need a constant supply of moisture for best growth and flowering. This doesn't imply keeping the plants soggy, for they need perfect drainage, but plants kept on the dry side show fewer new leaves and flowering is delayed.

Given fairly rich soil, geraniums will grow several weeks without additional nutrients. But for maximum growth they need feeding with an all-purpose fertilizer at biweekly intervals. Many hobbyists fertilize geraniums every week with a one-fourth-strength fertilizer solution. Under indoor conditions it is best not to try the foliar feeding methods with these plants as wet leaves can bring on troubles of mildew, rot, and botrytis. However you choose to fertilize your geraniums, always do so when the soil is moist. Fertilizer running through dry soil can burn feeder roots, stunting and, in some cases, killing the plant.

Pelargonium domesticum, the regal or Martha Washington geranium, requires different culture than its relatives, the common geraniums. Unless you can give it a cool, 60-

degree growing area, don't expect abundant flowering, although seedlings and cuttings propagate readily under lights. A Canadian friend has successfully grown some of these handsome pansy- and azalea-flowered pelargoniums under a pair of 74-watt fluorescents in a cool basement growing room. Stop pinching the tips of all domesticums after late December, otherwise the plant may not have time to develop buds for spring flowering.

Geraniums of any kind showing cupped-down leaves or puckered leaf depressions are not receiving enough light. To keep these plants in good form boost them closer to the light source, or add additional tubes. Weak growth and long spindly stems may also indicate that plants are not receiving enough light.

Most modern varieties of geraniums grown under good light do not need pinching to make them branch. However, if you think your plants are not growing as bushy as they should, pinch out an inch of the tips. This will make them branch out.

Many gardeners believe that geraniums prosper under near desert conditions with no special thought to humidity. This is a false supposition. If you want flowers you need to provide them with some humidity. With a reading of 40 per cent humidity, good light, soil, and watering, you can expect a showy display of flowers from your light-grown geraniums. But if you try growing them in rooms where humidity hovers between 15 and 20 per cent, don't expect a big flower show, no matter how much light you afford them.

Repot geraniums when roots start coming out of the drainage hole, or when the plants appear top heavy. Repot into pots but one size larger, always providing ample drainage. I have found they grow well in almost any type of pot —ceramic, clay, or plastic—just be sure there is a drainage hole.

Propagating Geraniums

Propagate geraniums through cuttings or seed. Four-inch cuttings taken in the fall and grown under lights will give you flowering plants for Christmas and into the next spring. You needn't dip the cutting into hormone powder, for geraniums root easily. If you want to use the hormone treatment, cut it down to half strength by mixing with talcum powder.

Root cuttings in sand, vermiculite, perlite, or a prepared mixture such as Black Magic. Advanced growers often root cuttings in soil, but I find with this practice a large percentage of cuttings fall prey to rot.

Plant cuttings singly in 2½-inch pots or plant several to a pan or flat. Cover the plantings with transparent plastic and set them about 4 inches from the light tubes. They will start into growth without the plastic, but it does conserve some of the moisture and, for me, it gets the cuttings off to a faster start. If moisture beads appear inside the plastic, remove it and wipe dry, then replace. Leave it on about a week, then gradually admit air by opening the plastic. Many cuttings root in ten to fourteen days and are ready for 3- or 4-inch pots within a month from cutting time. If you want to see how rapidly geraniums root, stick a cutting in water, set it under lights, and observe the roots as they develop.

It's great fun to grow geraniums from seed. Dealers stock all types—*hortorum, domesticum,* scenteds, and miniatures. To make the slender, hard-coated seed germinate more rapidly, remove the outer shell. Plant the seed in any of the growing mediums suggested in chapter 7. Press them into the surface, cover with about a quarter inch of the mixture, water the planting, and await germination. They do not need to be under lights during the germination period, but

I find it easier to check on them when they are among the rest of my plants. Geranium germination is irregular, with some seedlings appearing in four or five days, others waiting weeks before germinating. Geranium seeds are also long-lived, a fact I saw proven most effectively. In the winter of 1951–52 I did a considerable amount of geranium hybridizing in a small lean-to greenhouse on my parents' farm in western Oklahoma. Recently on a visit I found some packets of these seeds I had harvested more than a decade ago. Out of curiosity, I planted them, and germination was as rapid as that of recently harvested seeds.

Geranium seedlings grow rapidly and should be pricked out and planted into individual 1- or 2-inch pots of soil as soon as they can be handled.

Keep the seedlings as close to the lights as possible without actually letting the leaves touch the tubes. They will need another shift into 3- and possibly 4-inch pots, where they will flower.

To obtain seeds from your own plants, dust some of the powdery reddish-brown pollen from one flower onto the pistil of another. If the cross is successful the seed will ripen in about a month. Remove the husks and they are ready to sow.

If you are going to use light-grown geraniums outdoors (or even window-grown ones), harden them off before moving. Do this by placing them in a shaded, sheltered outdoor area for a few days before planting out in open beds, borders, and boxes.

Geranium Problems

Geraniums are subject to a host of ailments and insect problems. But proper culture, spacing of plants so that leaves of one do not touch another, and detailed attention to temperature, light, water, fertilizer, and sterilized planting soil will prevent most problems.

Nutrient deficiency symptoms, arising from lack of fertilizer, show first on the leaves. If young leaves stay bright green and older ones turn red, the plant may be in need of *nitrogen*. When geraniums lack *phosphorus* old leaves turn dull red, starting at the margins and progressing inward. Soon they dry and drop off. Lacking *potash*, young leaves become pale yellow-green and the older ones show dull yellow between veins. Correct diet deficiencies by using an all-purpose houseplant fertilizer at intervals suggested on the container.

Stem rot and cutting rot starting at the base and progressing upward evidence a disease for which there is no cure. It is usually spread from one plant to another through cutting knifes which have been used on infected plants. Destroy these plants, and pots, too, unless you want to go to a great deal of trouble using highly poisonous mercuric chloride solution to disinfect the pots. Disinfect cutting tools before using them on other geraniums.

Virus diseases such as leaf curl and mosaic, a showing of light- and dark-green leaf areas, have no cures either. Destroy old stock, propagate new plants from healthy stock. Fortunately, the commercial geranium growers are doing such a vigilant job of controlling diseases that you are not likely to find them in your collection.

Common pests which may attack house-grown geraniums include aphids, red spider mites, mealybugs, white flies, and nematodes (see chapter 8).

Geraniums to Try under Lights

With so many kinds of geraniums available locally and through specialists by mail, you will have no trouble finding types you like. In fact, my problem is quite the contrary.

There are single- and double-flowered hortorums with plain or zoned leaves; trailing ivyleafs, some with variegated foliage; deliciously perfumed scenteds, smelling of fruit, spice, mint, roses, and some as pungent as a pine tree; and there are dozens of miniatures, some that grow only 2 or 3 inches high in two years' time.

As difficult as it is to be highly selective with geraniums, I believe if I were limited to 24 for a fluorescent-lighted garden, these varieties would make up the two dozen:

Alpha

Antares

Appleblossom Rosebud

Carlos Uhden

Cuba

Formosa

Gold Rush

Grand Slam

Lady Luck

La France

Luster

Miss Burdett-Coutts

Mr. Wren

Mrs. Kingsley

Pink Poinsettia

Prince Rupert Variegated

Scarlet Unique

Single Rose-Pink Bird's Egg

Skies of Italy

Souvenir de Mirande

Strawberry Sundae

Tiny Tim

Velma

White Mesh

17

Cacti and Other Succulents
Have Stamina

The gardener who has little time to spend with his plants, yet wants to grow some unusual ones, will find a world of pleasure among cacti and other succulents. Here are plants with exotic flowers, and sometimes bizarre forms, yet all are so carefree they can be grown with a minimum of effort and time. While many of these plants are much too large for home culture, there are hundreds that will grow well under artificial light.

Succulents, plants with fleshy, moisture-storing leaves, stems, or tubers, have the ability to survive long periods of drought. There are succulents in many plant families. One example is the sweetheart geranium (*Pelargonium echinatum*), which, besides being a succulent, also has thorny stems. *All* members of the *Cactaceae* are succulents, but *all succulents* are not cacti.

Culture in Lighted Gardens

Contrary to common indoor-gardening practice, cacti should not be grown in hot, dry rooms, especially in the winter. Nor should they be grown too close to window glass. Ordinary window glass filters out or reflects many of the sun's rays, but most of the infrared and other harmful rays come through, to the plant's detriment. Controlled fluorescent light obviates this problem.

I like to grow spiny cacti such as neoporteria, a ball-shaped, winter-flowering cactus, and *Opuntia acicularis*, in a lighted glass cabinet. Here visitors, especially youngsters, can observe without danger of getting caught by the spines.

Cacti grow fairly well under a pair of 40-watt fluorescents, but they really outdo themselves when grown under a combination of fluorescents and an additional 10 per cent incandescent light. Give them sixteen to eighteen hours of artificial light daily. For a really successful under-light garden of cacti and other succulents, use a 48-inch fixture with four 40-watt tubes, one of these being daylight, one deluxe cool white, and two Gro-Lux or Plant Gro. Other plants that will thrive with this light setup include orchids (except this may be too much light for the paphiopedilums or cypripediums), geraniums, and miniature roses.

If you want cacti to flower, you will have to learn the flowering season for each species or variety and plan to give it at least three months rest before this time in a room where the temperature does not go above 60 degrees in the day. While resting they need light but the soil should be kept fairly dry. When new growth shows, the temperature can be raised to normal and the plants can be given regular watering and feeding. This period of coolness is not necessary for most succulents other than cacti.

If you are more interested in the curious forms than in having flowers, cacti need not be relegated to a cold room during the winter. However, most of them should be kept fairly dry from November until February or March, for this is a normal resting period for these plants.

Flowers for Christmas

If you want your Christmas cactus (*Schlumbergera bridgesi* and varieties) to bloom profusely for the holidays, it will be necessary to provide special conditions in late summer and early fall each year. At the end of the eighth month each year begin a period of eight weeks when your Christmas cactus receives only eight hours of illumination daily. If you don't want to set your automatic timer so that all your plants receive only eight hours light daily during this period, follow the plan of my friend, Dr. Sheldon Reed of St. Paul, Minnesota: His lights are turned on at about 7:30 each day, and when he returns home from work each afternoon, the Christmas cactus plant is transferred to a dark closet. The next morning before he leaves the house, the Christmas cactus is brought back to the lighted garden. This may seem like a lot of trouble, but it's a pleasant routine for any gardener, and the rewards are obvious when the arching branches are laden with flowers for the holidays.

Figure 6. Branch of Christmas cactus (*Schlumbergera bridgesi*).

The majority of cacti grow best in porous, alkaline soil. This is not difficult to mix, or you can purchase prepared soil by mail from cactus specialists. To mix your own, use equal parts of garden loam, sand (or perlite), and leaf mold. Add to it a half part each of chipped charcoal and oyster shells (you can buy these at poultry supply houses). This is the type mixture I use for desert cacti. For the epiphytic, jungle types such as *Epiphyllum* and *Schlumbergera,* I use a medium more like that for other tropicals such as the gesneriads: equal parts garden loam, peat moss, sand (or perlite), and leaf mold (or vermiculite).

Cacti grow best indoors in small pots. Transplant during

the growing season or right after flowering. Do not move budded cacti, even to display them in some other part of the house. A move at this time usually results in dropped buds.

Pests and Problems

If you must put newly purchased cacti in with your collection of other plants, give them a spraying with denatured alcohol, or a few whiffs from an aerosol of houseplant pesticide.

Cacti and other succulents are subject to many kinds of pests: mealybugs (especially), scale, nematodes, red spider mites, thrips, and aphids. Light-brown discolorations starting at the base of the plant and spreading upward may be caused by thrips or red spiders. For control measures, see chapter 8.

Withering or yellowing may be a signal to give the plant fresh soil, or it may mean the roots have rotted from overwatering. Remove the plant from its pot and trim away all dead root tissue. Repot in fresh soil, and water lightly until it becomes established. If soft rot appears on a plant, cut it back to firm tissue. Dry the cutting at least one week before repotting it.

Cacti for Beginners

If you are just starting to grow cacti, begin with the easy-to-grow, readily available kinds, then progress to the rarer types. 'Lady Fingers' (*Mammillaria elongata schmolli*), an old favorite, has harmless, bright-yellow spines. 'Ruby Dumpling,' a small mammillaria, has bright-red flowers and is easily grown. Thimble cactus (*Mammillaria fragilis*) is covered with soft white spines. Beginners are especially fond of this one because it produces so many offspring. 'Bishop's Cap' (*Astrophytum myriostigma*) is shaped as the common name implies. 'Silver Ball' (*Notocactus scopa*) is rounded and covered with silvery bristles. The strawberry cactus, another mammillaria, is a 3-inch green globe whose yellow flowers are followed by bright-red berries. 'Red Crown' (*Rebutia minuscula*) produces clusters of new plants each year. Red flowers appear in the spring and last for several weeks.

Cacti to Grow for Unusual Forms

The curiosity plant (*Cereus peruvians*) is indeed a curious plant. It is dark green with reddish-brown spines and slowly develops into a fan-shaped tree form. I like spineless living-rock cacti, all of which are varieties of *Ariocarpus*. 'Mexican Living Rock' appears to have dozens of leathery brown petals, topped with a wooly center. Its daisylike flowers are pink. The 'Crested Hedge Hog' (*Echinopsis multiplex cristata*) is the newest member of my collection. It is a fascinating plant with ruffled disks bending and twisting into curved grooves. Gnarled, twisted, green *Cereus hybridus* 'Monstrosus' resembles a coniferous bonsai. The 'Sand Dollar,' round and spineless, is aptly named, for it is like its namesake, the sea urchin.

Cacti with Showy Flowers

Most cacti have pretty flowers, but I like especially the Paramount Hybrids originated by Harold Johnson in California. The flowers on 'Peach Monarch' are 5 to 7 inches long and a small plant in a 2-inch pot often has as many as six flowers open simultaneously. 'Orange Glory' shows flat, 2-inch flowers. 'Aurora' has salmon-orange flowers with wooly tubes. 'Terra Cotta' is a beauty, with white flowers striped with reddish-orange. The current catalog from Johnson Cactus Gardens, Paramount, California, will bring you up to date on other hybrids similar to these.

Succulents for Lighted Gardens

The plants we call succulents assume many forms: narrow- or round-leaved, rosettes, small tree shapes, vines, and many more. Thick-leaved, neat haworthia is a member of the lily family. Rapid-growing dyckia, a plant with spiny green rosettes, is a bromeliad. The jade plant (*Crassula arborescens*), echeveria with its neat rosettes, and sempervivums, often called hen-and-chicks, are members of the *Crassulaceae*. Petite-leaved rosary vine (*Ceropegia woodi*) belongs to the *Asclepiadaceae* or milkweed family, and counts among its relatives the common roadside pest, milkweed. This is but a sampling of the hundreds of succulents from which you can choose. All have two things in common: They need a reduced water supply during the resting period, usually in fall and early winter, and all thrive under a pair of 40-watt fluorescents; most give even better results with four tubes as described earlier in this chapter for cacti.

When it comes to naming my favorite succulents for under-light gardens, it is hard to know when to stop, but here is a list of my favorites:

Crassula 'Morgan's Pink' and *C. triebneri*

Dwarf 'Crown-of-Thorns' (*Euphorbia splendens* 'Bojeri')

Echeveria pulvinata and *E. derenbergi*

Fenestrarias

Hoyas ("wax plants")

Kalanchoe eriophylla and *K. houghtoni*

'Little Joshua Tree' (*Sedum multiceps*)

Lithops (the "stone faces")

'Rainbow Bush' (*Portulacaria afra tricolor*)
Stapelia gettleffii
Titanopsis calcarea

I like to summer both cacti and other succulents outdoors in a sheltered area where they receive some protection from scalding sun at noontime. A lath house is fine, but if you don't have one, place the pots near larger plants where they will receive some shade, or on north-facing shelves mounted on fence or garden wall. If you live in an apartment, these luxuries may not be available, but don't worry. These plants will keep on growing in an artificially lighted garden all year.

Figure 7. The jewel plant (*Titanopsis calcarea*) is an easily grown succulent that stays about 2 inches tall when properly lighted.

Succulents for Planters

If you plan to use succulents in planter dishes, give them the benefit of one-third drainage material such as pebbles, charcoal, or broken pot chips. But don't expect these plantings to last as long as individually potted plants. The soil in the bowl should be a little heavier than that used for potting. (Substitute half garden loam for one part of sand recommended.) The heavier soil will help you anchor the plants easily and will not dry out as quickly as a lighter soil. Don't ever apply water carelessly so that the soil becomes soggy. Small plants and rooted cuttings are best for the bowls because they last longer. A sprinkling of charcoal over the topsoil will help keep it fresh. Include a few pieces of colorful rock to show off the plants.

Give your planter a good start under lights. When you need it for room decoration, treat it like a flower arrangement, taking it out into the living room for a few days, then returning it to the lights. You will find its useful life will double with this care.

I have some different plantings which you might enjoy making too. The base of the plantings is weathered wood which I have sprayed moss green. I hollowed out small areas just large enough for the potted succulents, set them in the wood, then finished the plantings with trailers such as rosary vine. A similar planter is made of driftwood. Here I have filled the natural holes or pockets in the wood with drainage material and potting soil, then planted these with sempervivums. In winter these plantings thrive under fluorescent light; in summer they decorate our outdoor living area.

Sempervivums, the popular houseleeks or hen-and-chicks, can be had in dozens of varieties. They are invaluable for neat borders, rock gardens, and dozens of garden designs. However, it takes quite a few of them to make a good showing. In our area all are hardy, but I have found that rabbits eat the small ones such as S. *allioni*. To combat this problem and to increase my crop of sempervivums, I remove many of the smallest offsets in the fall, pot them, and winter under lights providing the same conditions I give cacti. Seldom do they show growth from October to February. Then they take a real spurt and often send out several new offsets.

How to Propagate Cacti and Other Succulents

Propagate cacti and other succulents from cuttings, off-sets, seed, or by grafting. To take cuttings, use a clean, sharp knife, and make the cuttings during spring or summer. Heal the cuttings a week to a month in a dry, shaded place until the cut area is well calloused or shows a thickening of the "skin" at the base. Healing time depends on the weather. Cuts heal more rapidly in hot, dry times. Root cuttings in sand or perlite.

If you want to increase your collection rapidly and economically, grow some cacti and other succulents from seed. Specialists carry a wide variety, and it is possible to have dozens of these interesting plants from a single packet of mixed seeds. Among the succulents, particularly, you will find strange little plants, many of which bloom six months after planting. Seed-planting methods are detailed in chapter 7.

Learning to graft cacti can become a fascinating hobby. Grafting is used when you want a slow-growing cactus to make a showing in a hurry; to save a cactus when but a small piece is left after cutting away rot, or in some instances, where someone can supply you with but a tiny cutting of a rare kind; or when you want to obtain new forms. Make the graft when the part to be grafted (the scion) and the plant receiving the graft (stock) are making growth. The end of the scion is tapered, the top of the stock is cut to receive it, for the growing tissues must be united. Use rubber bands or cactus spines to hold them together. Keep the grafted plant in a warm moist place. When the stock and scion appear to have united and growth is obvious, remove the rubber band or cactus needles.

18

Miniature Roses for a Garden
under Lights

Miniature roses, colorful and charming, are diminutive rep-
licas of favorite landscape roses. These small beauties grow
only 6 to 12 inches high but they produce an abundance of
nickel- to quarter-size double or single flowers in favorite
rose colors—white, pink, gold, and red. Some novelty types
send flowers that open pale gold and finally turn to dark
rose-red. Many of these dainty roses are richly fragrant. All
can be adapted to under-light gardens.

Rose Culture in Lighted Gardens

Miniature roses can be grown successfully under a wide
variety of fluorescent light setups, or they can be grown at a
fairly bright window with supplementary fluorescent light.

Given optimum conditions as to soil, watering, feeding,
and temperature, you can flower miniature roses with sixteen hours of illumination from any of these lights with suitable reflectors: a pair of 40-watt agricultural lamps; one
agricultural and one natural; one daylight and one natural;
and under any combinations of white, daylight, or natural
74-watt tubes. One collector recommends using four 40-
watt tubes—a pair of agricultural tubes and one each of daylight and deluxe cool white for miniature roses.

Supplement natural light with 60-watt incandescents or single strip fluorescents, burning the lights on cloudy days and for at least four hours in late afternoon and evening every day.

A grower in Illinois has installed lights and ventilating fans in a glass case. Grown in a 60-degree basement recreation room, his miniatures flower the year around; daytime temperatures are higher, about 70 degrees, continuing into the evening until the family retires for the night.

Most miniature roses are hardy or near hardy, which means they may be able to survive winters where temperatures fall to 10 degrees above zero or below. In summer gardens they grow to unblemished perfection with the same care given hybrid tea roses.

Taking cues from these natural growing habits helps us select prime indoor growing conditions for miniature roses. They grow thriftily indoors in daytime temperatures ranging from 60 to 72 degrees, with the usual drop at night. Under high temperatures leaves shrivel and brown and buds may blast. In warmth and high humidity foliage and buds may develop naturally, but stems elongate too rapidly and soft, succulent growth results.

Now that we have our home centrally humidified, we are comfortable with the heat thermostat set at 68 to 70 degrees and the humidistat at 50 per cent relative humidity. Miniature roses fairly burst with blooms in this atmosphere. Admittedly, three small children let in an abundance of fresh air, much to the liking of miniature roses.

A well-drained, humusy soil made of equal parts garden loam, peat moss, and sand serves them well. Some experts advise mixing a level tablespoonful of garden lime with each pint of peat moss or leaf mold before mixing it with rose soil. I would not do this, however, except in a climate where the garden loam is strongly on the acid side.

Good drainage is imperative. Add pebbles or crushed crockery to the pot. Newly purchased plants, especially those arriving from mail-order firms, can be planted in pots one size larger than the original growing container. Trim off broken leaves and branches. After potting, give the plant a watering, then place it under the lights. A distance of 7 to 12 inches from the tubes will give you a general idea of placement. If plants show spindly growth, they need to be set closer to the lights or the lighting period needs to be extended an hour or two daily. If bushes push into the lights, move them away from the tubes or prune the tops of the plants. They respond to shearing with a heavy crop of new leaves and buds.

If the leaves on new plants seem particularly dry and curled, sprinkle them with water and slip a plastic bag over the plant before setting it under lights. As new leaves emerge, remove the plastic covering.

These miniatures grow best when soil moisture level is kept fairly high, but they soon die if roots have to struggle in puddly, soggy soil. Margaret E. Pinney, author of the excellent *Miniature Rose Book* (Van Nostrand, 1964) says that, after years of experience, she is sure that clay pots are better than plastic for these roses. After you have grown them for a while you can tell at a touch if the soil is moist enough. It should be as firm and springy as a moist chocolate cake.

Miniature roses growing under lights can be fertilized at biweekly intervals. Most growers like to alternate fertilizers, feeding one time with a special rose food or a soluble all-purpose fertilizer, and making the next feeding with an organic type such as Atlas Fish Emulsion or Liquid Blue Whale.

It is normal for roses to take a rest during November and December. This is the time to prune heavily, removing ungainly branches and cutting back others. Keep them watered but omit fertilizer during this period.

Miniature roses are subject to the same diseases and pests that bother big roses. Blackspot is the worst enemy. It can be controlled with special sprays or with a mixture of wettable sulfur and malathion. The malathion, of course, adds to this mixture insect control, while the sulfur acts as a fungicide. Figure the mixture in gallon proportions of each (directions are on containers), then cut the recipe down to the size you need. Spray every third day until the spots are gone, then give 10-day sprayings. Blackspot thrives on warm days followed by cool, damp conditions at night. You can help avoid it by never watering your plants in the afternoon or evening—only in the morning.

Once-a-week spraying with a houseplant pesticide aerosol will discourage or eradicate pests such as red spider mites and aphids, both frequent enemies of miniature roses. There are also all-purpose aerosols on the market offered specifically for roses. You may be able to use one of these that includes an insecticide and a fungicide for the push-button convenience and effective control of all pests and diseases.

If you have an outdoor garden, by all means summer your miniatures there. Prune them back and summer by sinking the containers in a protected garden area when danger of frost has passed. If you plan to make these roses a permanent part of the outdoor garden, remove them from the pots and plant as you would any other roses.

Potted miniatures need repotting at least once a year, either spring or fall. Remove some of the old soil from the rootball, and replant into the same pot or one size larger.

Some growers like to store potted miniature roses in a coldframe during the early part of the winter to give them a longer resting period. They take the plants out of the coldframes in late December and bring them into the house for winter flowering.

Propagating Miniature Roses

Propagate miniature roses by cuttings or seed. Cuttings will give you reproductions of your favorite varieties, but don't propagate patented varieties this way for resale. Seed produces a variable lot of plants which are easily grown under lights.

Take 3-inch cuttings in August or September from new growth. Cuttings made from old wood are difficult to root. Take strong growing shoots, dip the base of the cutting in a hormone powder such as Rootone. Insert several cuttings in a 6-inch bulb pan or plant them individually in 2-inch pots of vermiculite or a mixture of two parts gritty sand (or perlite) to one part of peat moss. Stick the cuttings an inch deep. If leaves start to wilt, mist them frequently with tepid water. Place 12 inches from the lights. Cuttings generally root in about four weeks. Transplant rooted cuttings to 2-inch pots of sterilized soil.

Seeds of baby roses (*Rosa polyantha nana*) are available from several sources. There is also a preseeded planter on the market which will give you dozens of these small roses. Seedlings are not usually fully double varieties, but they will bloom in seven to ten weeks from the time seeds germinate, yielding single and semidouble flowers in shades of white, pink, and rose.

To the best of my knowledge, no firm offers seed of the fully doubles. You may be able to make your own plants produce seed by removing pollen from one flower and placing it on the pistils of another. If you cannot find pollen on any of the doubles, use some from one of the baby polyanthas. You may have to make dozens of pollinations to obtain seed from the named varieties.

Press miniature rose seeds into any starting medium and cover lightly. Some will germinate in two or three weeks, but it may take two or three months for the entire batch. I had unusual success growing rose seeds another way. Add the seed to half an inch of water in a refrigerator dish or ice tray and put it in the freezer. Remove in two weeks and plant the seed in peat moss and sand, or your favorite seed-starting medium.

Transplant seedlings as soon as you can handle them. Thumb pots are fine for the first shift. These miniatures bud when they are but an inch or two high.

Named Miniature Roses

All leading rose growers carry a line of miniatures, some only a half dozen representing the major colors and types, and others, like Mini-Roses Nursery in Texas (see chapter 22) have as many as fifty or more. Ask for catalogs, then study descriptions and select colors and combinations that appeal most. Personally, I have grown at one time or another two or three dozen different varieties. These stand now as my favorite dozen:

Baby Betsy McCall	Polka Dot
Oakington Ruby	Scarlet Ribbon
Bit O'Sunshine	Orange Elf
Pink Joy	Thumbelina
Baby Gold Star	Yellow Bantam
Easter Morning	Bo-Peep

19

Spring Comes Early under Lights

Forced bulbs and branches brought into bloom ahead of the normal outdoor schedule bring a fragile and subtle air of spring to any room. Forcing paper-white narcissus and the related golden-flowered 'Soleil d'Or' is pure simplicity; success is assured. Amaryllis, too, with their great trumpets of snow-white or dazzling colors are sure to flower. Daffodils, hyacinths, and tulips require a little more work, but you will feel well paid when they unfurl all the glory of a fine spring day. Even the common iris—in its many sizes—can be forced into winter flowering under lights.

To force paper-white narcissus, fill a 3-inch-deep bowl or other container half full of pebbles or perlite. Place the bulbs on the porous material, leaving about a half inch of space between them. Pour in more pebbles or perlite until about one-third of the bulbs are covered. Add water to the container until it touches the base of the bulbs. Set the plantings in a cool (50 to 60 degrees) dark closet or basement area for about two weeks. It is fun to make at least one of these plantings in a clear glass container and watch the root growth. In about two weeks when root growth seems active, bring the plantings to your lighted garden. Here they will send up strong, straight stems, and when the flowers open there will be a delicious fragrance all around your indoor garden. Gardeners living in the South can replant these bulbs into outdoor gardens. The rest of us discard them after the blooms fade.

Plant other bulbs such as daffodils, tulips, hyacinths, and crocuses in October. A good soil mixture is equal parts garden loam, peat moss, and sand, with a heaping teaspoonful of bone meal to each 5- to 7-inch pot of soil.

A 5- to 7-inch pot will accommodate a varying amount of bulbs: three or four hyacinths or daffodils; two or three tulips; four to eight small bulbs such as miniature daffodils, grape-hyacinths (muscari), or crocuses. Plant bulbs so that soil covers the tips. Water the plantings. Cover with inverted pots and set in a coldframe or a trench that is about a foot deep. Leaves or hay placed under and above the pots, and wedged in-between them, provide insulation. Use boards to keep leaves from blowing away. An unheated garage may also be used for this cool period needed for root growth: group pots together, well moistened, and cover with burlap or tarpaulin; check frequently to be sure that the soil never dries out.

In late January transfer the pots to a cool closet or basement. Keep the bulb tops covered with paper cones or sacks until they are showing active leaf growth. Then move them to a warmer room and place under fluorescents. It takes about four to six weeks for the bulbs to bloom. Discard after flowering, or plant in the outdoor garden. They will bloom there in future years, but they will not be suitable for forcing again.

Amaryllis arrive in stores with huge buds already growing in them, and sometimes showing. Pot in well-drained pots of porous soil, leaving about an inch of space between bulb and pot. Leave at least one-third of the bulb above surface. Water and set under the lights. Artificial light holds down the height of the scape, but even so it is best to set these bulbs under adjustable setups for the scape may grow too tall otherwise. When the flowers wither, water and fertilize the plant to make it grow as many leaves as possible. (This helps it store food to grow next year's buds.) In the fall withhold water and fertilizer and set it in a cool closet

Countertop collection of cacti and other succulents lighted by two 40-watt fluorescents. The odd succulent *Bowiea volubilis* showing in right foreground has had its lacy green topgrowth trained around a giant cone. (SELECT STUDIOS)

Rhipsalidopsis rosea and *Schlumbergera gaertneri* are small-growing epiphytic cacti that are excellent for underlight gardens. (PHILPOTT)

Countertop lighted garden with tulips, Dutch irises, hyacinths, and daffodils forced into bloom with azalea which occupies a permanent place in the garden. (SELECT STUDIOS)

Miniature roses, from left to right, 'Bo-Peep,' 'Red Imp,' and 'Cinderella' grow readily under fluorescent lights. (STAR ROSES)

Robert Anderson's fluorescent-lighted Minnesota greenhouse from which came the first double pink African violets.

Greenhouse of Albert H. Buell, Eastford, Connecticut, where under-bench fluorescent lighting doubles the growing space. (GRUBE)

Countertop lighted garden of bromeliads, including rooted pineapple top, Spanish moss draped on trellis in background *(Tillandsia usneoides)*, *Aechmea fasciata* (far left) which has held its flower for several months, neoregelia hybrids, and low-growing earth stars (cryptanthus). (SELECT STUDIOS)

Sweet potato planted in attractive container of vermiculite and trained to unusual form under fluorescent lights.

Kaempferia decora is one of the showiest of all summer-flowering plants for lighted gardens. The crepe-textured flowers are lemon-yellow, about 2 inches across, borne in profusion day after day all season. (HOYT)

or basement. Sprinkle the soil with water about once a week so that severe drying will not occur. After four to eight weeks, or when new growth shows, bring your amaryllis back to the lighted garden for another growing season.

Our garden iris, too, can be forced into winter bloom. The dwarfs are best suited to under-light culture. Pot up some dwarf iris rhizomes in late October, choosing those which have made good seasonal growth. Do not use fans that have bloomed the previous spring. Pot in any reasonably good soil. Place them in a sheltered place such as under shrubs or next to the house foundation. Bring into the house in late December, place under lights in a setup where daytime temperatures do not go over 72 degrees. These plants flower in about six weeks. After flowering set the plants any place where they won't freeze, and moisten the soil occasionally. Replant in the outdoor garden when weather permits.

Marvelously fragrant freesias are tender bulbs that can be forced into bloom in a cool under-light garden. Purchase the corms in September. Plant in 6- or 7-inch pots containing a mixture of equal parts garden loam, peat moss, and sand. Keep evenly moist at all times, and position them first for a period of about six to eight weeks in a cool (50 degrees) dark place so that root growth can take place. Then bring them to a lighted garden where daytime temperatures stay below 70 degrees, and drop by at least 10 degrees at night. In these conditions the plants should make good growth and provide a season of fragrant flowers in midwinter. After the flowers are gone continue watering and feeding until about May or June. Then withhold water and plant food. When the foliage dies down, turn the pots on their sides in a dark dry place and leave in dormancy until replanting time the following late August or September.

Forced branches add a refreshing touch of spring to indoor gardens and arrangements. You can force them for foliage any time during dormancy, but if you want flowers wait until the buds swell on forsythia, lilac, cherry, plum, and pear trees. For greens use branches from any tree or shrub. Force them in any deep container, then transfer to prettier ones. Pebbles and a 2-inch layer of charcoal added to the water will keep it fresh. Cut branches 18 to 30 inches long. Trim away dead twigs. Place the branches in a tub of tepid water for twenty-four hours. Weight them down during this soaking. Then arrange the branches in a utility container or separately in a more ornamental one. Place under the lights and in a few days you will see green flecks dotting the branches and there will be buds and opening flowers before long.

Forced branches often grow a sturdy set of roots and can be transferred later to the outdoor garden.

Start Your Outdoor Garden under Lights

If you want a colorful garden of annuals, biennials, or perennials, start them ahead of time under your lights. Vegetables, too, respond to under-light conditions. It is possible to produce stocky, bushy petunia plants covered with flowers under eighteen hours daily light duration. Laboratory tests have proved that petunias grown under twenty-four hours continuous illumination flower year-round but bear only a few leaves. The other green parts—stems, sepals, and bracts—carry on photosynthesis.

Few of us are concerned with making such plants flower under light, but it is desirable to have them ready for garden planting when the soil is warm and danger of frost has passed.

Plant annual or vegetable seeds in pots or flats of vermiculite, sphagnum moss, perlite, or a finely sieved mixture of sterilized potting soil made of equal parts peat moss, garden loam, and sand. Packet directions will tell you how deep to plant the seeds. Cover plantings with glass or clear plastic. If you can keep your growing area at 60 to 70 degrees, you can raise excellent flowering seedlings with only a pair of 40-watt fluorescents. Four 40-watters are better for growing vegetables. Use any of the white combinations, or white and an agricultural tube, or a pair of agricultural tubes alone. Set the plantings about 6 inches from the center of the tubes. When seedlings elongate, move them farther from the lights. Pansies require less light. Place them at the end zones.

The gardener who likes compact, short-stemmed plants should light the seedlings ten hours a day and grow them cool—around 50 to 65 degrees. This delays blooming slightly but gives sturdy, short-stemmed plants about six to eight weeks after planting that are excellent for transplanting to the outdoor garden. If you want to hurry the plants along, grow at 70 to 75 degrees, and light them sixteen to nineteen hours daily.

Do not use incandescent bulbs on these seedlings as the red light emitted from incandescents tends to make seedlings spindly. In tests made at the George W. Park Seed Company, however, it has been found that petunias flower much better under fluorescents with the addition of some incandescent light.

Seedlings growing in vermiculite, sphagnum moss, or perlite need to be repotted into soil as soon as they can be handled. Otherwise, give these seedlings weekly feedings of one-fourth-strength soluble fertilizer such as Hyponex or Ra-Pid-Gro.

Easily grown long-day annuals include China aster, "bachelor's-button" (*Centaurea cyanus*), coreopsis, "forget-me-not," petunia, phlox, rudbeckia, salpiglossis, scabiosa, snapdragon, and verbena. The ten-hour day suits them best at the seedling stage.

Among the short-day annuals are cockscomb, cosmos, globe-amaranth, marigold, salvia, and zinnia. Seedling growth is best when lighted sixteen hours daily with fluorescents. But if you want to have some fun with a few of these (and you have more than one light setup) give them ten-hour light days and watch them flower on short stems.

You can handle seeds such as this in any of your lighted setups or you can make a special case with a hinged cover to hold the lights. When the cover is let down the humidity stays higher in the case. Suggested dimensions for such a case are 6 feet long, 3 feet wide, and 3 feet high. This case will use a pair of 40-watt tubes. You may want to vary the size. For instance, a case 3 feet wide might be too wide to slide through doors easily.

Make the case of moisture-resistant wood such as 1- × 2-inch pieces of redwood or cypress. A metal or plastic liner or tray will catch excess water and enable you to water the seedlings from the bottom (an important time-saving factor in the spring when there is more gardening to do than most of us have time). If you have your case in a cool, 50- to 60-degree room, you may need to install a heating cable to furnish additional warmth. If you use a soil-heating cable and plant directly into the case, add about 4 inches of rooting medium above the cable. Although heating cables are readily available through specialists and some dealers, you may want an electrician to install it in the case.

The gardener who wants to try just a few annuals or vegetables under lights will have fun growing preplanted gardens of petunias, marigolds, tomatoes, and herbs. You can purchase these at local garden centers, even at the supermarket, or by mail. With these preplanted gardens it is not necessary to assemble growing medium, buy seeds, or do the planting. All you do is add water and give them light.

When large enough, transplant as many seedlings of each kind as you will need into 2-inch pots of soil. Pots can be of peat or bagasse (with these you bury the pots in the garden at transplanting time without disturbing seedling roots), or standard clay or plastic containers. Harden the seedlings for at least a week (ten days may be better) before planting in the open outdoor garden. Even then it is wise to shade with a paper or some small branches the first few days in the garden, especially if you have unusually warm weather in that period.

Vegetable seedlings mature rapidly under lights. Asparagus, for instance, germinates in two weeks and three-day-old seedlings can be transplanted to 3-inch pots of soil.

Beets, broccoli, cauliflower, celery, cucumber, eggplant, peppers, and tomatoes are but a few of the vegetables that make speedy growth under lights.

Temperature for most vegetables should be cool, between 60 and 65 degrees, or even slightly lower. Cucumbers, squash, eggplant, and tomatoes are exceptions, for growth is accelerated when temperature is raised to a range of 65 to 70 degrees.

Tomatoes are among the favorite plants for starting indoors, but they grow so rapidly that really early planting is out of the question unless you have plenty of space. In our area tomatoes go into the garden from early to mid-May. I sow the seeds in late February or early March under lights, and transplant to individual 3-inch pots of soil in three or four weeks. With regular feedings they will grow to flowering size under lights. Like all other plants destined for the outdoor garden, tomatoes need a hardening-off period before making the abrupt change of hothouse to outdoor conditions. Small-growing 'Tiny Tim' cherry tomato may be cultivated the year around under lights; to initiate heavy fruit set, spray according to container directions with Blossom-Set (available at local garden centers and by mail from seedsmen).

Checking the dollar-and-cent situation, I am sure the grower who starts annuals and vegetables under lights saves some money, besides the great pleasure in having dozens of plants to put outdoors and to share with neighbors and friends.

Biennial and Perennial Flowers to Start under Lights

Biennials are plants that take two growing seasons to complete the cycle from seed to bloom and back to seed. Favorites are "Canterbury bells" (*Campanula medium*), English daisy (*Bellis perennis*), "foxglove," "sweet William" (*Dianthus barbatus*), hollyhock, and "forget-me-not."

All of these and other biennials can be started from seed in artificially lighted gardens. Plant seed as suggested for annuals, and grow in temperatures between 60 and 70 degrees.

One popular perennial that responds well to seed propagation under lights is the polyanthus primrose. Mrs. John G. MacDougal of Scotia, New York, writing in the winter 1965 issue of the *American Primrose Society Quarterly*, reports planting polyanthus seeds the first week of February after they had been refrigerated for seven months in a glass jar. She prepared flats with a mixture of equal parts garden loam, sand, and peat moss, adding a "handful of bone meal." This mixture was firmed and leveled, then topped with one-fourth inch of milled sphagnum moss. The seeds were sown and kept uniformly moist at all times. Mrs. MacDougal's seedlings appeared within a week, and they were positioned 3 inches from two 40-watt fluorescents burned fifteen hours daily in a temperature range of 65 to 75 degrees. In mid-March she gave each flat a week in a south window, then returned to the fluorescent light. The seedlings were fed every two weeks with deodorized fish emulsion. In mid-April the seedlings were transplanted to 2¼-inch clay pots and positioned in a protected coldframe. The project netted nearly six hundred plants of unusual root growth and all-around vigor for transplanting into the outdoor garden in mid-May.

The collector or hybridizer of perennials such as iris or

hemerocallis will get much satisfaction from growing these plants from seed. Plant the seed in any growing medium, water the plantings, and place anywhere under the lights. When growth shows, place the seedlings 6 inches from the center of the tubes. Daylily (hemerocallis) seeds begin to germinate in ten to fourteen days, and continue for several weeks.

Iris seeds are slow to germinate. Freeze the seeds by placing them in an ice-cube tray half filled with water. When the water freezes, fill the tray with more water. Plant the seed, ice cubes and all, after two to four weeks.

It is possible to have flowering iris and daylilies two years after starting them under lights. (This is based on a growing program with seedlings being started in early winter, then transplanted outdoors when the weather warms.)

One of my friends takes in small clumps of early-flowering *Hemerocallis minor* from the garden in late February, pots them, and forces early flowers under a pair of 40-watt fluorescents.

Of course you can start seeds of almost any other kind of perennial, shrub, or tree under lights too. See chapter 7 for more information on plant propagation.

Bulbs, Corms, and Tubers to Start under Lights

In addition to early spring bulbs for forcing under lights, there are numerous bulbs which put on a grand show under two or more 40-watt fluorescents. Many of these are members of the amaryllis family and require the same general culture. *Sprekelia formosissima*, haemanthus, and zephyranthes are easily cultivated and give lovely flowers. Sprekelia has showy red blooms with slender, twisted petals. There are several haemanthus which make truly exotic additions to indoor gardens. *H. katherinae* has a globular head of hundreds of tomato-red flowers. Personally, I prefer *H.*

multiflorus for my indoor gardening. Its growth is neater, the scape stays at about 8 to 10 inches under lights, and the flower head is as round as a ball. Oblong leaves about 6 to 8 inches long flank the red-dotted flower scape.

Zephyr flowers or rain lilies (zephyranthes) are obtainable in white, pink, red, and yellow varieties. Pot them in the fall (August to November), placing four or five bulbs in 5-inch pots of loam, peat moss, and sand. Plant the bulbs 3 to 4 inches deep. If you are crowded for space you can start these in any warm growing area away from the lights, then place them under the lights when the green shoots push through the soil. Water and fertilize regularly while active growth continues, then dry off. After a short rest, resume watering. Shortly thereafter flowering should occur. You can repeat this routine over and over with zephyranthes. Propagate by removing offsets.

Cyrtanthus, a small-growing amaryllid, is one of my favorite plants, one that can be depended upon for elegant blooms every late autumn and early winter. Basically the culture I give, as to planting time and aftercare, is the same as for zephyranthes except that I keep cyrtanthus in constant growth, drying off only in September. Watering is resumed again in about eight weeks, followed shortly by the annual flowering season.

Some gladiolus hobbyists start corms under lights to be transferred later to the outdoor garden. I never seem to have space for starting mature corms and I do not feel that those started indoors bloom much earlier than those planted directly in the garden. But the hybridizer will find fluorescents useful for starting seeds or growing on small corms.

Tuberous begonias, dahlias, and caladiums can be started into early growth under lights. In fact, tuberous begonias and caladiums can be grown as permanent plants in lighted gardens.

If you have named varieties of dahlias you want to spur into early growth, start them under lights in late February.

Remove all but two or three of the sprouts when they are about 2 inches high. Dip the ends of these in rooting powder and root them as suggested for any other cuttings (see chapter 7). The new plants, and the old tuber, too, will be ready for the garden when the weather is warm enough for planting out.

Tuberous begonias, caladiums, and dahlias can be started in a pan or small flat of any propagating material—vermiculite, perlite, sphagnum, or peat moss. Light, porous soil containing at least one-third part of peat moss also makes good starter material.

A Herb Garden under Lights

Growing herbs is one of the most fascinating of garden pursuits and several popular kinds can be grown well under lights. They do not attain quite the firm-textured growth they do in the sunshine outdoors, but the leaves are aromatic, and, if you don't want to make the herb garden a permanent under-light feature, start some of them from seed as suggested for annuals in this chapter.

Chives, which you can purchase in clumps from many grocery stores, are as satisfactory under lights as in the outdoor garden, and it is a culinary treat to have fresh chives to add to salads and other food.

Parsley, which often languishes on windowsills, grows thriftily in a cool 60- to 70-degree fluorescent-lighted area. The leaves have rich green coloring and are fine for garnishing soup or meat.

Watercress is easily grown indoors under lights. It likes plenty of fresh, clean water. The first time I grew some I transplanted seedlings to regular soil, but found they needed so much water that the pots had to be standing in it much of the time. Now I grow watercress a much easier way. I add a half inch of crushed charcoal to the bottom of small pots, an inch or more for larger containers. The pot is filled with perlite and the cress is transplanted from seedbeds into these individual pots. The perlite holds moisture longer than the potting soil. The plants are fertilized weekly and I keep a fresh lot of seedlings coming along biweekly, for it grows rapidly under lights. Even the small leaves are flavorful and will be ready for nipping two weeks after sowing.

Other herbs to try under lights are sweet basil, borage, chervil, sweet marjoram, and sage. The ornamental sage (*Salvia officinalis*) 'Tricolor,' with pink and white markings on gray-green leaves, is an excellent choice for under-light gardening. Pineapple-sage (*S. rutilans*), too, is a special treat from the herb world, and quite manageable under fluorescent lights.

20

Greenhouse Gardens to Grow under Lights

If your greenhouse is bulging at the seams and you would like to change dark under-bench areas into lighted growing ranges; if you need day-extenders to lengthen short winter days so you can bloom out-of-season long-day plants; if you need cyclic lighting to hold back the blooming of short-day plants; if you want to grow both shade and sun-loving plants; or if you would like to hasten a hybridizing program, consider the advantages of adding artificial lighting to your greenhouse.

The Best Light

If your greenhouse is overcrowded and your under-bench area hasn't sufficient light to grow or propagate plants, you may be able to double or triple your growing area by installing fluorescent lights. Selecting fluorescents for the greenhouse depends first on the space you have to fill. If the plants you will be growing in the lighted area depend entirely on artificial light, allow 15 to 20 watts of fluorescent light per square foot of growing space. If you have a 100-inch-long under-bench area to illuminate, choose two 74-watt fluorescents rather than the 40-watters. The larger lamps are more efficient than pairs of 40-watters installed end to end. To illuminate a wider growing area, add strip tubes. Space the 40-watt types about 2 inches apart; the 74-watters 4 inches apart.

Whenever possible enclose electrical wiring for greenhouses in half-inch conduit and use moistureproof outdoor fixtures and switches.

Lamps with a high percentage of red in them are most effective in turning short days into long days. Both incandescents and warm-tinted fluorescents such as Gro-Lux are practical.

Incandescent bulbs are often used in greenhouses to lengthen days. Use lamps with reflectors to force the light down on the plants. Space between the plants and lights is determined by the size of the bulb. A 25-watt incandescent and its reflector mounted so that the bottom of the reflector is about 2 feet above the plants will give about five foot-candles of light to a bench that is 3 feet wide. A 75-watt bulb with reflector about 4 feet from the bench will light an area 6 feet wide. For additional foot-candles space 25-watters 3 feet apart; 75-watt bulbs 6 feet apart.

In addition to increased or decreased light, temperature, too, has a role to play in the flowering time of some plants. Petunias, for example, flower at 63 to 75 degrees with long days, and at 55 degrees irrespective of day length. But they do not flower at 63 to 75 degrees with short days.

These findings were reported by Robert and Struckmeyer (1939), but I checked them out myself the last three years when I needed a bountiful supply of petunias to add quick color to the garden of our new home.

Before adding lights to your greenhouse, ascertain the electrical load your circuits will carry. Local power companies usually offer free consultation in matters such as this.

To increase the efficiency of the lights installed in underbench areas, paint shelves white for better reflection, use fluorescents with added reflectors, or, if these seem too ungainly for the area to be lighted, check on fluorescents with built-in reflectors. These reflector fluorescents have built-in metallic reflectors covering about two-thirds of the tube circumference.

Controlled Day Length

Scientists have learned that many short-day plants such as chrysanthemum and Japanese morning glory, for instance, can be restrained from flowering by the application of one minute of twenty-five to fifty foot-candles of light during the middle of twelve-hour dark periods.

Long-day plants can be persuaded to flower by short light periods applied in the middle of twelve-hour dark periods.

It is possible also for the primary flower parts to be formed during one type of day length and for the flower to develop and bloom in another type of day length. The China aster (*Callistephus chinensis*) is a good example of this. For years growers have disputed the day length of this plant. Now scientists believe the China aster forms flowers and rosette elongation during long days. When short days are given this plant directly after the leaves of the rosette begin to lengthen, the rosette stops growing and flowers come along much sooner than if it had continued receiving long days.

Strawberries form buds during short days, and flower during long days.

Long-Day Plants

Long-day plants are rather intermediate in their reaction to additional light. Many of them will flower more rapidly when grown under high temperatures.

Some of the plants which benefit from long days are bouvardia, calceolaria, centaurea, cineraria, clarkia, digitalis, feverfew, heather, and nasturtium.

Short-Day Plants

Reduce the day length on short-day plants by darkening them a part of each day to lengthen the night and hasten flowering. Heavy black sateen, black plastic, or building paper may be used. Put the plants under cover at about 5 P.M. daily and remove the covering at 7 A.M.

Some commonly grown short-day plants are begonia 'Melior,' bougainvillea, chrysanthemum, poinsettia, and Christmas cactus.

While the commercial grower finds it profitable to produce crops at off-season, the home grower may find it stimulating to experiment with the effect of shortening or lengthening the days to produce flowers for arrangements, to have annuals flowering in advance of the neighbors, or for spurring growth on specimen show plants.

For Complete Illumination

The duration of the light depends on types of plants you grow; green plants manage nicely on four to ten hours daily, depending on how rapidly you want to increase growth. Flowering plants and seedlings need twelve to sixteen hours of fluorescent light daily.

If your greenhouse glass extends nearly to the soil level so plants under benches receive some natural light daily, eight hours of fluorescent light during the evening may be enough to grow seedlings of African violets, begonias, gloxinias, and foliage plants, coleus for example.

The home greenhouse grower will appreciate most the addition of lights to give him more space to grow and flower additional plants. The grower who likes to have sun-loving plants as well as shade-loving types can satisfy the needs of both by growing plants such as geraniums, cacti, and tropical fruit in sunny benches. Shade-loving plants—African violets, begonias, and others—can be grown under the benches in artificially lighted areas.

Artificial light offers a way to increase propagating space too. A corner in a potting area, a wall shelf, or an area near the floor (as well as any other space available in the greenhouse) can be lighted and used for propagation. Cuttings, seedlings, tubers—all will be spurred into rapid growth under lights.

Adhere to the same basic culture you have found successful for growing your favorite plants and with the added advantage of artificial light you will always have a greenhouse brimming with flowers and dozens of new plants coming along in the propagating area.

With the aid of lights in the greenhouse, dozens of professional hybridizers and hundreds of home hybridizers are able to bring seedlings to bloom more rapidly.

African violets are a notable example of this. Robert Anderson, Minneapolis, Minnesota, owner of Tonkadale Greenhouses, carries on much of his hybridizing work in an artificially lighted greenhouse (see photo 30). One proof of the effectiveness of this program: Through his accelerated growing procedure, Mr. Anderson was able to get his double pink African violets (the first ever offered) on the market in advance of other professional growers.

Light also speeds the growth of seedlings such as *Aechmea fasciata, Anthurium scherzerianum,* begonias, cacti, and other succulents, all gesneriads (including gloxinias), kalanchoe, miniature roses (other kinds of roses, too), and ferns.

Unusual Greenhouses

Most of us buy or build our greenhouses of wood or metal and encase them in glass or plastic, but an increasingly large number of growers have discovered the value of greenhouses constructed from used fluorescent tubes. While the average hobbyist is not likely to use enough light tubes to build a greenhouse, these spent tubes can be obtained from large commercial firms who must dispose of them after the useful light life is over.

I saw handsome orchids, African violets, and begonias growing in a Tulsa, Oklahoma, greenhouse made of fluorescent tubes. Several California growers have designed tube greenhouses and lath houses. Here, in addition to the above plants, some hobbyists include ferns, amaryllis, and epiphyllums.

Small lean-to houses can be made from 96-inch tubes. Larger houses can be made by placing 96-inch tubes end to end in a framework. Corrugated fiber glass makes a good roof. Ventilation areas such as a Dutch door and a vent in the roof must also be included in the structure. There was a time when fluorescent tubes were filled with highly poisonous gas. Now they are coated inside with a powder. They can stand quite rough treatment before breaking and should one break while you are making a greenhouse, handle the shattered material as you would any other broken glass.

If you want an air-tight tube house, you will have to devise some method of caulking between the tubes. If not, there will be minute spaces between the tubes, but water seldom runs into the house, it simply trickles down the tubes. Tube houses never need shading.

Dr. A. Garnett Richardson, a retired chemist whose plants and light setups had reached undesirable proportions in his home, built a greenhouse complete with fluorescent lighting for day-extending and built-in cisterns for wick-watering his plants.

The cisterns, made of eleven 4 × 8 × 16-inch cement blocks, hold about 9 gallons of water. These are set in the ground under benches. Three large wicks of fiber-glass cloth tubes filled with fiber-glass wool reach from the bottom of the cistern up through openings in the bottom where they are frayed out and sewed to a fiber-glass cloth bench lining. Smaller aluminum reservoirs are placed on the undersides of wall shelves with smaller fiber-glass wicking running to the plants on these shelves. Wicking helps keep the soil constantly moist, but never soggy. The reservoirs also add additional humidity to the greenhouse.

This greenhouse is lighted by pairs of 40-watt agricultural lamps installed end to end on either side of the greenhouse above the benches. An incandescent fixture is installed between each pair of fluorescents. Wattage of the incandescents varies from small ones used to break the night cycle to 75-watters for highlighting a specimen plant.

A greenhouse gardening friend in Texas says that, although she doesn't particularly need artificial lights to add growing space, she uses a few of the Gro-Lux lights in her greenhouse to call attention to it in the evening. She writes, "It is surprising how many people, seeing the plants under these lovely pink and lavender lights, want to find out what they are and how they, too, can use them."

21

Mix or Match Under-Light Gardens

There are countless ways to create colorful and fascinating under-light gardens. If your budget cannot be stretched to include expensive plants, you can design an extravagant-looking garden with a frame of foliage, centered with a mass of ever-blooming plants—wax begonias, impatiens, or African violets. You can even grow novelty gardens from the seed and tops of some fruit and vegetables.

If you lack space, concentrate on miniature plants. There are diminutive African violets, gloxinias, cacti and other succulents, roses, orchids, ivies, and oxalis—to name a few. For a change of pace, grow a forest of fake bonsai from rapid-growing tropical seedlings such as citrus, *Harpephyllum kaffrum* or *Delonix regia.* Or, you might make a collection of the bizarre and sometimes beautiful bromeliads.

The addition of a single new plant such as hibiscus, anthurium, red-fruited ardisia, rivina, or ornamental pepper, used as a focal point, will make your entire garden take on a new look.

Plants in these decorative gardens can be grown in any good growing soil such as equal parts peat moss, garden loam, and sand, in average living-room temperatures. To keep plants in peak condition, fertilize biweekly during the active growing season. Two, three, or four 40-watt fluorescents will shed ample light for good growing. Burn the lights ten to sixteen hours daily, depending on whether yours is a garden of foliage or flowers alone, or combines foliage as well as flowering plants.

Figure 8. Anthurium clarinervum is a handsome foliage plant for a lighted garden that is warm and humid.

A Pink and Red Garden

One of the most stunning under-light gardens I have ever seen was based on a monochromatic color scheme of red and pink. Papery thin pink-leaved caladiums bordered the back, single-flowered pink wax begonias edged the sides. The center was a mass of double, red-flowered wax begonias.

Equally exciting would be a background of pink- and green-leaved coleus framing red-flowering begonias or impatiens.

You can even add a sun-drenched, spring look to under-light gardens with yellow-flowered *Oxalis cernua,* a small-flowered bulbous plant, and yellow-green coleus 'Chartreuse' with geraniums like 'Cloth of Gold.' Dramatize a green and white garden with a center or edging of ruby-leaved bloodleaf (*Iresine herbsti*).

Pink and violet combinations have stimulating appeal.

Pink-flowered *Oxalis rubra* is charming when intermingled with violet-flowered achimenes, African violets, or gloxinias. It's a real knockout when grown as a companion for purple velvet plant (*Gynura aurantiaca*). To keep gynura compactly shaped, start pruning when the plant is young. This helps it grow bushier.

No-Cost Gardens

Vegetables and fruit can yield novelty plants of interest to adults and children alike. You can grow a handsome gray-green foliage plant from the top of a pineapple. Cut off the top, leaving a small slice of fruit attached. Plant in moist growing soil. I have a year-old plant that is 2 feet across. With luck, in another six months, we may have our own pineapple!

Glorious green vines can be grown from sweet potatoes (*Ipomoea batatas*). Most have been treated to prevent sprouting, so start with a tuber that shows sprouts. Plant vertically or horizontally, sprouted side up in soil, vermiculite, or perlite. Or insert the lower half in a glass of water and some charcoal. Change the water weekly.

You can grow a beautiful indoor tree from an avocado seed. Plant the large seed with the small end up, a half-inch below the surface of soil. Or you can insert toothpicks around it and root the lower end in a glass of water and transplant later to a regular growing medium.

Pomegranate seeds germinate quickly and make dainty-leaved greenery. You can buy a single-flowered dwarf variety, *Punica granatum* var. *nana*, which will flower and fruit under lights.

Citrus seed—orange, lemon, lime, and others—yield glossy leaved plants. They take years to flower and bear fruit, but along the way you can derive immense pleasure from the attractive, evergreen foliage. If you want fruit-bearing types in a hurry, buy the dwarf forms. They can be depended on to flower and fruit under lights, although you may have to help by cross-pollinating the blooms, transferring the powdery pollen onto the stigma when it is sticky.

Even the tops of carrots set into moist sand or vermiculite and placed under light soon sprout dark-green ferny leaves —an excellent project for the tricycle crowd.

Space-Saving Miniature Gardens

Plant specialists carry miniature forms of most of our favorite houseplants. If you have a passion for growing or collecting many different kinds of plants, but lack space to display them properly, consider collecting miniatures.

With miniatures you can make diminutive landscapes or dish gardens; or you can design a replica of a woodland garden or a desert scene. Display these tiny treasures in the smallest of pots, even thimbles. With careful culture you can grow many of these small beauties in glass or ceramic containers—goblets, sugar bowls, small pitchers, strawberry barrels, and stacked candy jars.

Culture of miniature plants duplicates that of average-size kinds, but they do need smaller pots. If you grow them in containers that lack a drainage hole, add a generous layer of crushed pot chips and a sprinkling of charcoal to the bottom of the container.

FAVORITE MINIATURE PLANTS FOR
UNDER-LIGHT GARDENS

Achimenes	Allophyton
Acorus	Alternanthera
Adiantum	Astrophytum
Adromischus	Bertolonia
Aglaonema	*Billbergia morelli*

Caladium humboldti
Calathea
Carissa
Ceropegia woodi
Chamaeranthemum
Chlorophytum bichetii
Conophytum
Crassula
Cryptanthus
Cyrtanthus
Dionaea
Echeveria
Echinopsis
Episcia dianthiflora
Euonymus japonicus microphyllus
Exacum
Faucaria
Ficus radicans and *F. repens*
Fittonia
Gasteria
Geranium
Hatiora
Helxine
Homalomena
Hoya bella
Hypoestes

Kalanchoe 'Tom Thumb'
Lithops
Lobelia
Lobivia
Malpighia
Mammillaria
Maranta
Monanthes
Notocactus
Oxalis
Pachyveria
Parochetus
Pellionia
Peperomia
Pilea
Plectranthus coleiodes
Portulacaria
Punica granatum nana
Rebutia
Rhipsalidopsis
Rose
Saxifraga sarmentosa
Scilla violacea
Sedum
Selaginella
Siderasis
Sinningia pusilla
Stenandrium

Bonsai-Style Gardens

Bonsai is a Japanese term used to describe artificially dwarfed potted plants, or the process used to train these plants. In Japan there are gnarled, aged trees probably less than 12 inches high, yet one hundred years old. These living,

Figure 9. Plectranthus coleoides has unusual variegated foliage, and grows easily under lights.

growing, works of art are handed down from one generation to another.

Such bonsai are not for sale. If you admire the art and wish to start a bonsai for future generations, please refer to the publications suggested in the source materials that follow this chapter. However, you can make realistic adaptions in the bonsai manner by purchasing and repotting rapid-growing tropical trees and shrubs or starting them from seed. Choose low, squatty containers (there are those made especially for bonsai), trim roots to fit the container, set the tree so it is centered or mounded above the rim of the container. Train it to shape by wrapping soft copper wire around the stems and bending to suggest plants that have been molded to interesting form by the elements of nature.

Figure 10. Bonsai collection, attractively displayed on teakwood stand. Plants include, upper left to right: *Ficus benjamina, Chamaecyparis obtusa pygmaea,* and *Zelkova serrata* (gray-bark elm); lower left, *Pinus thunbergii* (Japanese black pine). A cool, moist, well-ventilated fluorescent-lighted garden makes an excellent place for bonsai work.

Here are some of the plants I have enjoyed using in bonsai-type gardens: *Bauhinia variegata, Camellia japonica, Carissa grandiflora,* Citrus, *Ficus diversifolia, Grevillea robusta, Jacaranda mimosifolia, Nicodemia diversifolia, Pittosporum tobira,* Poinciana 'New Dwarf Yellow,' Pyracantha, *Schinus molle, Trachelospermum jasminoides.*

Bromeliads for Exotic Splendor

Bromeliads, strangely beautiful epiphytic (air) plants, have stiff leaves which whorl into flat or spired rosettes. Foliage varies from gray to green to maroon and bronze with in-between shades and contrasting stripes, mottling, or vividly colored centers and tips.

Flowers on some bromeliads are as richly colored as the foliage, and often exceptionally long lasting. *Aechmea fasciata*, the urn or living vase plant, has sea-green leaves marked with frosty white bars. Flower spikes are beautiful and long-lasting with pink bracts mingling with bright-blue flowers which finally turn to purple and rose. Flowers last three to five months and even the dried spikes make exciting additions to dried arrangements. There are dozens of other upright species, some with flowers followed by bright berries. The catalog of Alberts & Merkel Brothers (see sources in chapter 22) abounds in common as well as new and unusual bromeliads.

Cryptanthus or earth stars have flat rosette growth with stiff leaves and small flowers. 'Silver Star' (*C. lacerdae*) is emerald green with a bright-silver band down the center. These and other bromeliads are nearly immune to pests, they grow in low to bright light intensity, and are propagated easily by the removal of offsets. While they can be grown in regular potting soil, many hobbyists add one part charcoal to each pot of soil. The pots should be small, just large enough to keep the plant balanced. I have been successful with the unusual and highly colorful *Neoregelia carolinae* 'Tricolor' potted in plain unmilled sphagnum moss.

A single bromeliad will add new interest to a collection of foliage plants. A collection will give you a dazzling indoor garden that requires very little attention.

Center-of-Interest Plants

Foliage plants of all kinds grow to luxuriant beauty under lights. Even the common heart-leaved *Philodendron cordatum* takes a new lease on life as the space between nodes shortens and the leaves overlap in graceful profusion. But less common foliage plants such as *Cissus discolor* (really fantastic coloring under Gro-Lux!), maranta, *Rhoeo spathacea*, and crotons can become showpieces for under-light gardens. *Dracaena goldieana*, all kinds of hoffmannias, *Scindapsis pictus argyraeus*, *Anthurium crystallinum*, and *A. clarinervum* are other unusual foliage plants that put on a dramatic show under the lights.

Center-of-interest flowering plants for under-light gardens, sometimes overlooked because they are unusual, or one-of-a-kind types, include the popular shrimp plant (*Beloperone guttata*), with bronzy bracts, and its variety 'Yellow Queen' for bright chartreuse-yellow accent, and *Crossandra infundibuliformis*. *Kaempferia roscoeana, K. rotunda,* and *K. decora* are among the showiest of all summer-blooming plants for lighted gardens. There are other kaempferias too. You might enjoy collecting them for an exciting summer garden under the lights. Wyndham Hayward (see sources in chapter 22) is the only retail grower I know who specializes in these interesting plants.

For flowers and foliage accent, there are two plants I recommend highly for under-light gardens: *Hibiscus rosa-sinensis cooperi* and *Fuchsia magellanica gracilis variegata*.

When you turn on the switch of your first fluorescent-lighted garden, you will have begun one of the most interesting pursuits of your life. No matter how common the plants may be that you elect to grow, the wonders of nature will happen every day right before your eyes. And beyond always lies the ever-increasing world of plant materials suited to phytoillumination. The hundreds of names mentioned in this book represent thousands of others waiting to be discovered, possibly by you, for under-light gardens.

22

Sources to Further Your Pleasure in Fluorescent-Light Gardening

SOURCES FOR LIGHTING EQUIPMENT

(Fluorescent tubes, reflectors, switches, and time clocks can be purchased through most electrical dealers or from large mail-order concerns. If you want special agricultural lamps, portable lighted carts, or specially designed, lighted plant-growing units, consult any of the firms listed here. Some are manufacturers who will direct you to a local source of supply. Others are mail-order firms with whom you can deal direct.)

Craft-House Manufacturing Company, Wilson, New York 10706 —Lighted plant stands.

Floralite Company, 4124 East Oakwood Road, Oak Creek, Wisconsin 53221—Fluorescent fixtures, mist sprayers, tubes, timers, trays, labels and other equipment; supplies also.

General Electric Company, Lamp Division, Nela Park, Cleveland, Ohio—Manufacturers of fluorescent and incandescent lamps.

House Plant Corner, P.O. Box 810, Oxford, Maryland 21654— Lighted plant stands, other equipment, and all kinds of supplies.

Lord and Burnham, Irvington-on-Hudson, New York 10533— Fluorescent-lighted Planetarium.

Neas Growers Supply, P.O. Box 8773, Greenville, South Carolina 29604—Table-top Gro-Lux units, other equipment.

Park, George W., Seed Co., Inc., Greenwood, South Carolina
29646—Fluorescent Gro-Lamps, other equipment, and supplies.

Shoplite Company, 566 Franklin Avenue, Nutley, New Jersey
07110—Fluorescents, incandescents, in regular and special
sizes.

Sylvania Electric Products, Inc., 60 Boston Street, Salem, Massachusetts 01971—Manufacturers of all types of fluorescent
lights, including Gro-Lux agricultural lamps.

Tube Craft, Inc., 1311 West 80th Street, Cleveland, Ohio 44102—
FloraCart, other lighting equipment, and supplies.

Verd-a-Ray Corporation, 615 Front Street, Toledo, Ohio 44102—
Manufacturers of Plant-Lites and fixtures.

Westinghouse Electric Corporation, Westinghouse Lamp Division, Bloomfield, New Jersey—Manufacturers of fluorescent
lamps, including Plant-Gro.

SOURCES FOR PLANTS TO GROW UNDER LIGHTS

(The price of the catalog, if known, follows the type of
plants sold. In all cases a five-cent stamp will be appreciated.
If you ask questions, it will be a good idea to include a
stamped, self-addressed reply envelope.)

Abbot's Nursery, Route 4, Box 482, Mobile, Alabama 36609—
Camellias.

Alberts & Merkel Brothers, P.O. Box 537, Boynton Beach, Florida
33435—Orchids and other tropicals. 25¢

Antonelli Brothers, 2545 Capitola Road, Santa Cruz, California
95010—Tuberous begonias, gloxinias, and achimenes.

Ashcroft Orchids, 19062 Ballinger Way N.E., Seattle 55, Washington—Botanical orchids.

Bart's Nursery, 522 Fifth Street, Fullerton, Pennsylvania—Bonsai
materials.

Buell, Albert H., Eastford, Connecticut 06242—African violets,
gloxinias, and related plants.

Burgess Seed and Plant Company, Galesburg, Michigan 49053—
Dwarf fruit and other houseplants.

Burnett Brothers, Inc., 92 Chambers Street, New York, New York
10007—Freesias and other bulbous plants.

Burpee, W. Atlee, Company, Philadelphia, Pennsylvania 19132;
Clinton, Iowa 52733; and Riverside, California 92502—Seeds
and bulbs.

Cook's Geranium Nursery, 712 North Grand, Lyons, Kansas
67544—Geraniums. 25¢

Conrad-Pyle Star Roses, West Grove, Pennsylvania 19390—Miniature roses.

DeGiorgi Company, Inc., Council Bluffs, Iowa 51504—Seeds and
bulbs.

DeJager, P., and Sons, Inc., 188 Asbury Street, South Hamilton,
Massachusetts 01982—Bulbs for forcing.

Farmer Seed and Nursery Company, Faribault, Minnesota 55021
—Dwarf citrus and other houseplants.

Fennell Orchid Company, 26715 S.W. 157 Avenue, Homestead,
Florida 33030—Orchids.

Field, Henry, Seed and Nursery Company, Shenandoah, Iowa
51601—Houseplants and supplies.

Fischer Greenhouses, Linwood, New Jersey—African violets and
other gesneriads.

French, J. Howard, Baltimore Pike, Lima, Pennsylvania 19060—
Bulbs for forcing.

Goedert, Robert D., P.O. Box 6534, Jacksonville, Florida 32205—
Amaryllis, cyrtanthus, and other bulbous plants, especially
those from South Africa.

Green Acres Nursery, 14451 Northeast Second Street, North Miami, Florida 33161—Palms.

Hausermann's Orchids, Box 363, Elmhurst, Illinois 60128—Unusual species orchids.

Hayward, Wyndham, 915 South Lakemont Avenue, Winter Park,
Florida—Unusual tropical bulbs, including amaryllis, caladium, kaempferia, and others.

Hilltop Farm, Route 3, Box 216, Cleveland, Texas—Geraniums
and herbs.

Howard, S. M., Orchids, Seattle Heights, Washington 98063—
Miltonias, odontoglossums, and allied cool-growing genera.

Ilgenfritz, Margaret, Orchids, Monroe, Michigan 48161—Orchids.

Jones and Scully, Inc., 2200 Northeast 33rd Avenue, Miami,
Florida 33142—Orchids and other tropicals.

Kartuz, Michael J., 92 Chestnut Street, Wilmington, Massachusetts
01887—Houseplants, many bred especially for fluorescent-
light culture. 50¢

Lager and Hurrell Orchids, 426 Morris Avenue, Summit, New
Jersey 07901—Botanical orchids.

Logee's Greenhouses, 55 North Street, Danielson, Connecticut
06239—All kinds of houseplants, including rare and unusual
kinds. $1.00

Lyon, Lyndon, 14 Mutchler Street, Dolgeville, New York 13329
—African violets.

McLellan, Rod, Company, 1450 El Camino Real, South San Fran-
cisco, California 94080—Orchids and supplies.

Merry Gardens, Camden, Maine 04843—Complete selection of
houseplants. $1.00

Mini-Roses, Box 4255, Station A, Dallas, Texas 75208—Miniature
roses.

Nies Nursery, 5710 Southwest 37th Street, West Hollywood, Florida 33023—Palms.

Nuccio's Nurseries, 3555 Chaney Trail, Altadena, California 91002
—Camellias.

Park, George W., Seed Co., Inc., Greenwood, South Carolina
29646—All kinds of houseplants, seeds, bulbs, and supplies.

Reasoner's Tropical Nurseries, Inc., P.O. Box 1881, Bradenton,
Florida—Tropicals.

Rivermont Orchids, P.O. Box 67, Signal Mountain, Tennessee—
Orchids.

Spidell's Fine Plants, Junction City, Oregon 97448—African violets
and other gesneriads.

Stewart, Fred A., Inc., 1212 East Las Tunas Drive, San Gabriel,
California 91778—Orchids and supplies.

Tinari Greenhouses, 2325 Valley Road, Huntington Valley, Pennsylvania 19006—African violets, related plants, supplies and
equipment.

Tropical Paradise Greenhouse, 8825 West 79th Street, Overland Park, Kansas 66204—Houseplants, supplies and equipment. 50¢

Wilson Brothers, Roachdale, Indiana 46172—Geraniums and other houseplants.

Yoshimura Bonsai Company, Inc., 200 Benedict Avenue, Tarrytown, New York 10591—Bonsai and supplies.

Ziesenhenne, Rudolph, 1130 N. Milpas Street, Santa Barbara, California 9303—Begonias.

SOURCES FOR POTS, SOIL, AND OTHER SUPPLIES

(Every supermarket carries a considerable line of the commonly used materials, and local garden centers have an even wider range. However, if you cannot get out, cannot find what you want locally, or enjoy the convenience of shopping by mail, these sources are suggested. You will note, also, that some firms listed under "Equipment" and "Plants" also stock supplies for lighted gardens.)

Greeson, Bernard D., 3548 N. Cramer, Milwaukee, Wisconsin 53211—Supplies. Catalog 10¢

South Shore Floral Company, 1050 Quentin Place, Woodmere, New York—"Mister" that creates foglike spray for increasing humidity around plants; fits in any soft drink bottle.

Sponge-Rok Sales, 7112 Hubbard Avenue, Middleton, Wisconsin 53562—Perlite.

Volkmann Brothers Greenhouses, 2714 Minert Street, Dallas, Texas 75219—General supplies.

Wilson Brothers, Roachdale, Indiana—Tropic-gro Planter and self-watering strawberry jars.

Yoho & Hooker, Box 1165, Youngstown, Ohio 44501—Pots, labels, and other supplies.

PERIODICALS AND PLANT SOCIETIES OF INTEREST TO UNDER-LIGHT GARDENERS

African Violet Magazine, quarterly of the African Violet Society of America, P.O. Box 1326, Knoxville, Tennessee 37901.

American Camellia Journal and Yearbook of the American Camellia Society, P.O. Box C, Tifton, Georgia 31794.

The Begonian, monthly publication of the American Begonia Society, 10934 East Flory Street, Whittier, California 90606.

Bulletin, monthly publication of the American Orchid Society, Inc., Botanical Museum of Harvard University, Cambridge, Massachusetts 02138.

Bulletin, bimonthly of the Epiphyllum Society of America, 4400 Portola Avenue, Los Angeles, California 90026.

Geraniums Around the World, quarterly publication of the International Geranium Society, 1413 Shoreline Drive, Santa Barbara, California 93105.

Gesneriad Saintpaulia News, bimonthly publication of the American Gesneria Society and Saintpaulia International, the Indoor Gardener Publishing Company, 1800 Grand Avenue, Knoxville, Tennessee 37901.

The Gloxinian, bimonthly publication of the American Gloxinia Society, Mrs. Diantha Buell, Secretary, Eastford, Connecticut.

Journal of the Cactus and Succulent Society of America, bimonthly, 132 West Union Avenue, Pasadena, California.

The National Fuchsia Fan, monthly publication of the California National Fuchsia Society, 13801 Shoup Avenue, Hawthorne, California.

Plant Life, annual of the American Plant Life Society, P.O. Box 150, La Jolla, California 92038.

Under Glass, bimonthly for home greenhouse gardeners, P.O. Box 114, Irvington-on-Hudson, New York.

INDEX

Abutilon: propagation, 66; white flies, 80

Acacia: propagation, 66; seed planting, 71–72

Achimenes, 99, 196; propagation, 68

African Violet Magazine, 104, 210

African violets, 32, 33, 35, 38, 98–110, 195, 196; "boy" types, 103; compatible plants, 85; containers, 54; cyclamen mites, 77; discovery, 121; diseases, 109; fertilizing, 105; flowers, 103–4; 108; gesneriads, 99; "girl" types, 103, 105; in greenhouse, 192; humidity, 107; hybrids, number of, 100; hybridizing, 191; indifference to day length, 18; leaves, cleaning, 107; light, 11, 13, 17, 23, 32–33, 40, 41, 99 ff, 105–6, 113, shock treatment, 110; miniature, 87, 195; -orchids, 144–45, 149; outdoor garden, 42, pesticide 114; pests, 108–10, control 81; phytoillumination, 104–5; from preseeded planters, 69; propagation, 60, 61, 64, 65, 108; saintpaulia, 100; seedlings, 190; seedpods, 70; shade, 191; soil, 106; specialists, 106; species, number of, 100, and hybrids, 100–104; temperature, 106, 107; under glass, 10; under-light culture, 106–8; 47; ventilation, 47; watering, 44, 45, 107

African Violet Society of America, 10, 107, 210

Agey, Wallace W., 9

Aglaonema, 85, 88

Agricultural lamps, 20, 25–26, 27, 89, 123; African violets, 104, 105; cost of tubes, 29

Air-layering, 68

Air plants, 90–91. *See also* Bromeliads

Alberts & Merkel Brothers, 202

Albrizzia, seed planting, 71–72

Allard, H. A., 18

Allophyton, 88

Alocasias, propagation, 63

Alpine garden, 123

Amaryllis: culture, 183–84; forcing, 175, 176–77; in greenhouse, 192; growing from seed, 70; propagation, 64, 68–69; soil, 56

American Begonia Society, 210

American Camellia Journal and Yearbook, 210

American Camellia Society, 210

American Gesneria Society, 210

American Gloxinia Society, 124, 210; founding, 13

American Orchid Society, 10, 145, 210; *Bulletin*, 143, 144, 145, 147, 210

American Plant Life Society, 210

American Primose Society Quarterly, 182

American Rose Magazine, 10

Amorphophallus, 90

Anacharis (elodea), 89

Angstrom, defined, 20

Annuals: case, 180; long-day, 18, list, 179; short-day, list, 179; temperature, 180; under lights, 178, 179–81

211